Looking Back
A Pilots Memoir
by Fred Phillips
Compiled by Elyse Cole and Hazel Phillips

Looking Back : A Pilot's Story
© Frederick Augustus 2015

All rights reserved. No part of this publication may be reproduced, stored in a retrieval system, or transmitted in any form or by any means, electronic, mechanical, photocopying, recording or otherwise, without the prior written permission of the author.

National Library of Australia Cataloguing-in-Publication entry

Creator:	Phillips, Frederick Augustus, author.
Title:	Looking Back : A Pilot's Story / Frederick Augustus Phillips; compiled by Elyse Cole and Hazel Phillips
ISBN:	9780994193704 (paperback)
Subjects:	Phillips, Frederick Augustus. Qantas Airways--Employees--Biography. Air pilots, Military--Australia--Biography. World War, 1939-1945--Aerial operations, Australian. Air pilots--Australia--Biography.
Dewey Number:	155.4124

Published by Frederick Augustus with the assistance of InHouse Publishing
www.inhousepublishing.com.au

CONTENTS

Memoirs Of Frederick A. Phillips 5
Official Bomber Command Losses 6
World War II 1941 Joining Up 6
1942 Parafield South Australia 8
Uss Tasker H Bliss Under Attack: 12
Wellington 1C Bombers — Oxfordshire, 1943. 18
July 1943 19
Toughening Up Course At Whitley Bay, S
heffield, North East England 1943 20
Stirling Conversion Unit, Stradishall, August 1943 22
Bandit In The Circuit 23
Stirlings 622 Squadron (3 Group) Mildenhall September 1943. 24
Stirling Operations September 1943 25
Mine Laying In The Baltic October 1943 26
Mannheim – Ludwigshafen November 1943 28
Stirling To Berlin November 1943 29
Lancasters November 1943 30
Stuttgart, February 1944 31
Nuremberg 31
Warboys, Pathfinder Force March 1944 33
No. 7 Squadron (8 Group) Pathfinder Force April 1944 33
Karlsruhe Pathfinder Force April 1944 38
D-Day, June 5Th 1944 40
Flying Bomb Site Oisemont Pathfinder Force, June 1944 43
Caen, Pathfinder Force, July 1944 43
Homberg Pathfinder Force, July 1944 43
Normandy Battle Area - Pathfinder Force, August 1944 44
Stettin In Poland, Near The East German Border About Sixty Km In
From The Baltic Sea Coastline – Pathfinder Force, August 1944 47

Stoney Cross, September 1944 50
Dc3'S Montreal To Sydney, 1945 53
Dc3 Dakotas In The Pacific —
No 243 Squadron Raf Camden, 1945 55
Medical Evacuations From Aitape, New Guinea 1945................................56
1945 – Ve Day..56
Vj Day, 1945 57
'Paddy', 1945 59
Qantas Empire Airways, 1946 61
Qantas, 1948 63
A Typical Day From Townsville To Lae, Ng Follows: 64
New Guinea, 1949 67
1950..69
1951..71
1953..73
War Egypt – Isreal (First War) 1954 74
Our Route At The Time Of The Diversion
To Beirut Was As Follows: 75
Qantas 1954 75
Sister Vivienne Bullwinkle 75
1954 Sir Edmund Hillary 76
Koalas 76
Qantas Check And Training Section, 1956..76
707 Training — Seattle, 1958 80
Fgy Pty Limited, 1960 85
Mervyn Richardson, The Victa Lawnmower Man.....................................86
Frederick Augustus Phillips: July 2014 Family History. 92
The planes I flew during my career as a pilot. 101

MEMOIRS OF FREDERICK A. PHILLIPS.

FLIGHT LIEUTENANT, R.A.A.F.
D.F.C. & BAR
CROIX DE GUERRE & LEGION OF HONOUR
PACIFIC STAR: AIRCREW EUROPE STAR & CLASP
PATHFINDER FORCE BADGE: 1939 – 1945 STAR
BOMBER COMMAND MEDAL

As my father, grandfathers, and great-grandfathers left not a single written word to relate their life and times to their descendants, I have put together an account of my life that I hope will be of some interest to those who follow me.

I was a Pathfinder and Master Bomber operating with the RAF. I completed sixty-four operations (51 of which were double tours with Path Finder Force (PFF). I commenced bombing operations with 622 Squadron at Mildenhall, where the England/Australia (London to Melbourne) race commenced.

A little background to this race, which was also known as the MacRobertson Trophy Air Race, is that it took place in October, 1934 as part of Melbourne's Centenary celebrations. Sir Macpherson Robertson, a confectioner, after whom the race was named, contributed a prize of $75,000. The Royal Aero Club organised the race and it ran from RAF Mildenhall to Flemington Racecourse, Melbourne; a distance of 11,300 miles (18,200km). We stayed at Mildenhall from September 1943 to March 1944.

I was then moved to 7 Squadron from April to September 1944. Of the sixty-four operations, fifty-five were completed on Lancasters and nine were completed on Stirlings. The biggest raid we ever controlled comprised of 1,250 four-engine bombers.

OFFICIAL BOMBER COMMAND LOSSES

Approximately 125,000 crew were trained at Operational Training Units (OTUs) and Conversion Units during the Second World War Total aircrew casualties amounted to 73,741 (almost 60%) of which 47,268 were killed in action and 8,232 killed in flying or ground accidents. The enemy shot down and took prisoner a further 9,938 with the remaining 8,403 wounded in flying or ground accidents and in aircraft that returned from flying operations.

It is estimated that the bomber command casualties amounted to almost one seventh of all British deaths in action by land, sea, and air from 1939 to 1945; British deaths, being a combination of all forces from the UK, Canada, South Africa, Australia and New Zealand.

WORLD WAR II

1941 JOINING UP

As soon as I turned eighteen I enlisted in the RAAF, in August 1941. I joined the rest of the potential aircrew, attending night classes at South Yarra High School. After the night classes we headed over to Adelaide to start our flight training. Everybody was hoping we would be able to cope easily. We were all very serious about becoming pilots.

Three months later, my mother was at Spencer Street Railway Station to see me off to Somers for initial training. Somers Training Camp, situated on the western shore of Western Port Bay, overlooked Philip Island. That was November 1941.

At Somers, we had intense training in math, navigation, Morse code, flight theory, meteorology, gunnery, physical training and, of course, marching.

On the 8th December, 1941, Prime Minister John Curtin declared Australia was at war with Japan, which meant all Defence establishments had to be guarded. In mid-December, another trainee and I were deposited on the beach of Western Port Bay, late at night with rifles and bayonets — no ammunition or lights, not even matches — to guard the beach. However, we had been well drilled in the current sentry challenge, 'Halt! Who goes there? Friend or Foe?' If the reply was 'Friend', next came 'Advance One and be recognised.'—Very simple – it reassured us both no end. (I think not!). No moon and absolute darkness made it a very long vigil. We were finally relieved at 2 a.m.

Of course, this was all very scary. The Japanese had a marvellous reputation for conquering everything they touched. First Hawaii, then straight after they had a brilliant win at Manilla – they knocked out the whole airbase in one go. The Japanese had built up a fantastic image of invincibility due to their destruction of Pearl Harbour and their rapid advance in S.E. Asia. I think all Australians were as alarmed as we were at that time.

Joining up 1941

1942 PARAFIELD SOUTH AUSTRALIA

Although my mother and I had been through so much together after my father died, it was plain excitement going to catch the train – interstate travel had not progressed very far then. There would have been around a hundred or so men there that day. You had to laugh — one chap, his father was an undertaker, arrived in a funeral car.

This airfield was where I first learned to fly DH82 Tiger Moth planes in early 1942. The DH82's were painted bright yellow. I had always admired the DH82; they were such good-looking planes. It was quite a remarkable feature to be among the first ones to travel such tremendous distances. About the only drama at Parafield was during an early flight with my instructor; the ailerons locked up while we were doing aerobatics over the Spencer Gulf. For safety reasons he suggested that I should bail out. The sea looked most uninviting so I said I would stick with him. He did a remarkable job of getting the plane on the ground with the use of rudder and elevator only.

My eldest sister, Sylvia, was to be married in Adelaide to Dr. Arthur Smith (who was also our station Medical Officer) and I was to give her away at the church in the early afternoon. I was flying solo that morning and had to do a forced landing in a paddock due to engine failure. I waved to a friend who had seen my emergency landing and he eventually landed in the same paddock. I explained the position to him and he agreed to let me fly his plane so that I could make the wedding. I arrived just in time to take Sylvia's arm at the entrance to the church.

Taking Mumma to Sylvia's Wedding

During my time training in Parafield, I saw my first Javanese pilots. They had escaped before the Japanese overran the East Indies (now Indonesia) and were continuing their flight training at Parafield. After finishing Tiger Moth flying in Adelaide we proceeded by train to Melbourne for pre-embarkation leave, then by train to Sydney to await a troop ship. To keep us occupied, each day we would march, armed with shovels – from Bradfield Park pre-embarkation depot to Lane Cove Park. We would dig holes in the morning and fill them in each afternoon. That was in May 1942.

In Sydney, I was staying with a young woman who I cannot now remember how I met. She lived in Mosman with her mother. I think all the mothers back then were keen to get their girls interested in pilots. This is where I was the night the Japanese midget submarines entered the Harbour and I heard the sound of big explosions for the first time.

On 31st May 1942, a fleet of five Japanese submarines, comprising three midget submarines and their two mother ships, arrived off the coast of Sydney in the Tasman Sea. The three midget submarines were sent to raid Sydney Harbour, which at the time was crammed with Allied shipping. Two midgets made it past the anti-submarine boom across the Heads ('The Heads' are the north and south heads to the entry of Sydney Harbour) – the third became hopelessly entangled in the net and the two men inside subsequently committed suicide by detonating explosives onboard.

The other two midgets made their way to Garden Island Naval Base. A torpedo fired at the American cruiser USS 'Chicago' missed its target, hitting instead the HMAS 'Kuttabul'; a former Sydney ferry converted to a navy stores ship. The ferry sank immediately, drowning nineteen naval ratings asleep on board. One of the submarines was hit and found at sunrise – the other disappeared. Sydney's Eastern suburbs residents became highly alarmed by the raid and a large number hastily headed west to the Blue Mountains.

There was great difficulty getting aircrew away from Australia, as there were submarines and sea raiders in most of the oceans. Eventually we travelled to Brisbane on troop trains. Continually shoved into dozens of sidings, to let the fast trains through, we were a kind of 'ring in'. We had nowhere to sleep, and it took days. I've forgotten how long, exactly, this journey took, however, we all got to know each other — we had to, we were going to be on a ship for seven weeks.

Our transport to the USA : "Tasker H Bliss"

On the 23rd June 1942 we travelled by bus to the wharf in Brisbane where we boarded an American ship called USS 'Tasker H. Bliss'. It soon became clear we were going to have to clean it up. The ship was in a hell of a state, particularly the latrines. However, because we did the latrines, we were given a choice of where we wanted to sleep — bunker or hammock. We all chose the hammock as it made it easier for us to sleep on the rolling ship. Thankfully none of us became sick, as we had been doing Tiger Moth flying, we had already had our turns with motion sickness — I was one of the lucky ones, I did not have to clean up the planes after those training sessions. This ship of around 10,000 tons carried our group of aircrew from Brisbane to Norfolk News, Virginia.

We journeyed south of New Zealand and for the next few weeks were in the most appalling weather and giant seas. Every evening just before dark a very American accent made the announcement – 'Now hear this. Lights Out. Blackout. Close all ports and do not smoke on the open deck'. This announcement was followed by the playing of the only record on board, 'Somebody Else Is Taking My Place' on side one and 'I Threw a Kiss in the Ocean' on side two. (To this day my family, on occasion, make the 'Lights out'... announcement prior to turning off lights at bedtime).

On board the 'Tasker H. Bliss' there were some (six, as I recall) mental cases whose cabins were just above the water line. On fine days, they exercised on deck, each having a leather collar around his neck, attached with approximately twenty feet of light chain. About a week before we reached Panama one of those poor devils managed to squeeze through a porthole and throw himself into the Pacific Ocean. The call went up 'Man Overboard', and we eventually stopped. The Captain was unhappy to be in such a dangerous position. We had seen some sharks in the water a short while before the man went over; needless to say, he was not recovered or seen thereafter. These men, we were told, had gone insane while building an airfield in New Caledonia.

Our first sight of land after leaving New Zealand was the Eastern End of the Panama Canal. As the ship had to be victualled and serviced we had a week to see both Colon and Balboa at opposite ends of the Canal. The Panama Canal was always something I had wanted to see. It was rather vast compared to what I had thought. All my mates felt much the same. A small train line ran beside the canal and took us away for the day. I did not drink at the time, but some of the fellows got sloshed. They did not know the drinks and there were bars all over the place. We quickly learned that the Panama Canal does not go straight across; it actually goes at an angle from east to west. Another fact that is remarkable is that there is about a six-foot difference (1.83m) between the heights of the ocean. On one side you had the cold current and on the east side you have the warm current, which comes down from the Gulf of Mexico.

We then crossed the canal, again in the 'Bliss'. We left Panama in a slow convoy to cross the Caribbean. This was, at the time, one of the hot spots for the U-boat packs. Food for the UK was coming from Argentina and this was one of the 'starve them out' policies of the German Navy. Although we slept on deck at night, our living quarters were forward and deep below the water line.

USS TASKER H BLISS UNDER ATTACK:

I was down in the living quarters one day when a sub attacked the convoy and some depth charges exploded only a half mile away. The noise below decks was incredible. I wasted no time in getting on deck to see what was happening. A Catalina flying boat was dropping depth charges and there were rumoured claims of a U-boat sinking. All of us were assigned lookout posts throughout the day and night.

In the Caribbean convoy, the ships were close together and around the outside bustled the oldest Destroyers we had ever seen. They were WWI four funnel jobs – coal fired – they belched huge amounts of black smoke. After being mothballed for so many years, they were finally sold to the UK by the US in exchange for some Islands in the West Indies, which had belonged to Britain. We often wondered whether their guns worked (fifty of these Destroyers were used to protect convoys). In the convoy when the Commodore sounded one toot, all ships would alter course to port, two toots and everyone turned starboard. This was going on at irregular times during the day and night. On one occasion, two toots and the tanker ahead of us turned to port and another ship quickly rammed her. The tanker leaked fuel oil continuously, which must have been a big help to the U-Boats.

We detached from the convoy and went to Guantanamo Bay, Cuba — to this day it still functions as an American naval base. The weather was fine, sunny, and hot. No sooner had the anchor chain stopped running than a number of us were in our underpants and diving over the side into the cool green water. After many weeks at sea looking at the bow wave, the height above the water seemed to be much less, and it was the highest dive I have ever experienced (thirty feet or so). The water had a greenish tinge; you could see the anchor go down and nestle in the sand. It was the clearest water. It was just too much for me. I had never done a dive like it. I nearly went legs over. It was absolutely marvellous jumping in; then the captain got on the blower and there was a mad scramble for the Jacob's ladder when the he loudly informed us that the Bay was full of man-eating sharks and barracuda. I'm pretty sure I lead the mob on this occasion but I paid for my folly as they had me working on the stainless steel pots with a big block of sand soap and metal mitts. I had to go right round the pot; they were about six feet deep and about four feet across. I just sweated like mad, stuck in the bowels of the ship, in the tropics. I had kitchen duties for the rest of the trip.

We eventually landed at Newport News, Virginia, a big US Naval ship building port. We were all happy to disembark from the 'Bliss' to board a train and proceeded to New York. Unfortunately the 'Bliss' was later sunk during the American invasion of North Africa.

We arrived at the famous Penn Station and made straight for the Empire State Building, which at the time was the tallest building in the world. Coming from Melbourne where the tallest buildings were eight storeys, the seventy-five or so of the Empire State was unbelievable. So was the view from the top balcony where we could see the huge French passenger liner, 'Normandie', on her side in the dock area. She had caught fire, rolled over, and sunk. Sabotage was suspected, as she had just broken the trans-Atlantic Blue Riband for the fastest crossing. We boarded a very luxurious train with sleepers and white jacketed attendants. We left for Montreal, arriving seven weeks after leaving Brisbane. At Montreal we divided up and I went to fly 'Harvards' at Dunville, on the shores of Lake Erie, Ontario.

It was here that I saw my first snow and learned to ice skate when all the rivers and ponds froze solid. We would go down to Buffalo and Niagara Falls on weekend passes – no trouble crossing the border to the US.

My first experience of snow

It was also in Dunville that we were inoculated. Normally when forming up for inoculation, we were called in alphabetical order. This day it was not so; they started with me — a double injection. After I was dosed, they realised a mistake had been made as one injection was from the wrong bottle. I became very sick; developing boils in my armpit, they took me off flying duties. They must have been thoroughly mixed up as they never did find out what combination caused the boils under my arms.

As unfortunate as my sudden illness was, it turned out to be rather fortunate, in a way. Everyone had gone out on a navigation exercise, a particularly difficult manoeuvre. An un-forecasted snowstorm caused absolute havoc and most of the men were hopelessly lost. The whole thing was a nasty experience and it took days to find everyone. Two Canadian pilots on our course died during training. You could not really navigate; all you could do was reverse your course. One fellow realised he was over one of the great lakes and just kept flying until he could see the lights on in the American towns; he bailed out over America. Some of them elected to fly low to see if they could see the ground; I cannot believe there were not more casualties.

After getting my Wings at Dunville in November 1942, we went to Halifax, Nova Scotia, in the middle of winter. The train journey was very slow due to snowdrifts. I had never experienced anything like the damp cold of Newfoundland. We were never conscious of actual temperatures as we are today with radio and TV weather reports. The bay at Halifax was frozen over and we skated on hired skates well out to sea (stupidly but fortunately uneventful). I recall spending a very dull Christmas in Halifax.

Having obtained my wings
Aged 20

There were thousands of Canadian troops and airmen like us, waiting for ships to go to the UK. Most left in a convoy but the Australian aircrew and some Canadian troops went on the RMS 'Andes', a rather large and extremely fast ship making for an unusual solo dash of ten days. Rumour had it that there were 15,000 troops packed into her. For all the advancements of the ship, the experience was basic at best. Quartered way below the waterline we only saw daylight for about an hour each day. We also had only two meals each twenty-four hours. We landed at Greenock on the Clyde near Glasgow, Scotland, on 8th January 1943.

On arrival we immediately boarded trains and travelled south overnight, arriving in Bournemouth the next day. Here they farmed us out in small groups to large guesthouses along the seafront. Our first night in town was a revelation as the darkness, due to the blackout, was complete. No streetlights - nothing. It was quite a job to find your way back to the guesthouse late at night, particularly in mid-winter. It was never dull, going to a town like London, for example, finding your way around was most difficult. It beat me how the local people even found their way. One would think there would be an increase in the rate of crime in darkness like that, but if there were, we were unaware of it and if there was any crime, they would have come down on it very harshly.

An old uncle of mine was the managing director of Phillips and Co, big importers of alcohol and Bristol Cream Sherry was one of their products. Beautiful sherry. My father was supposed to look up my uncle in WWI, but he had not. So my mother said that if I had an opportunity, I should go find him while I was there. Unfortunately I did not get the chance to see him, as he had been killed in a bombing raid on Bournemouth.

There was the odd intruder air raid and during the day we would see the contrails high in the sky where there was obviously fighter activity. Although I trained for single engine fighters, at this phase of the war (the Battle of Britain had long finished), there was little need for fighter pilots but a greater need for bomber pilots.

I flew Tiger Moths from Fairoaks, a small grass airfield in a beautiful part of England, near Reading, west of London. This was to give navigators from Canada and Australia practice in map reading over England having only known the wide-open spaces of our home countries; so vastly different from the tremendous amount of map detail found in the UK. The hundreds of roads, villages, railways etc., called for special skills to locate positions.

" THE LUCKY CREW:
Back Row : Self, Pilot / Dave Goodwin, Navigator (Nav 2) / Clive "Thirsty" Thurston, Radar and Fr. Gunner / AJ Harper, Specialist Bomb Aimer
Front Row: Stan Williamson, Radio Operator / Tom Jones, Flight Engineer / Ron Wynn, Mid Upper Gunner / Johnny Naylor, Rear Gunner

At this time in Fairoaks, I flew a New Zealander, Dave Goodwin, around a few times and we later met up on Wellingtons. He became my Navigator. It was necessary for me to convert to twin-engine aircraft and I trained on 'Airspeed Oxfords' in Oxfordshire. From there I progressed to Wellington bombers, also twin-engined. It was necessary to have a crew to fly Wimpeys (as the Wellingtons were affectionately known; named after the hamburger-eating 'Wimpey' in Popeye cartoons).

Pilots, Navigators, Observers, Wireless Operators, and Gunners were all released in a big hall. Dave Goodwin spotted me and had with him a friend, Clive Thurston, 'Thirsty', also from New Zealand. 'Thirsty' became the Front Gunner and Bomb Aimer. We collared an Australian Wireless Operator — Stan Williamson from Sydney — and we all four chose a 'nuggetty' young Englishman as our rear gunner — Johnny Naylor from Melton Mowbray in Leicestershire. We all had great difficulty with his North Country accent. These four men and I were to become the basis of The Lucky Crew...

WELLINGTON 1C BOMBERS — OXFORDSHIRE, 1943.

Many crews lost their lives on operations and in training on the Wimpey, as the slightest spark or tracer bullet, belly landing or collision (both, in the air or on the ground) would set the dope-stretched canvas alight and it would go up like the Hindenburg. The geodetic basket holes were not large enough for a person to escape through and because of its complete basket constructed framework there were a minimum number of exits. Even the pilots sliding side windows had bars on them as the propeller tips were within a few inches of the glass. What it meant was that one could not get out easily. Also the 1C had another limitation in its inability to feather propellers. Feathering allowed the blades to be turned edge on to the airstream in the event of engine failure, thus preventing windmilling which causes tremendous drag and subsequent loss of height.

JULY 1943

There was to be a first thousand-bomber raid on Cologne and in order to make up the numbers to get to the thousand bombers they pressed into action men from the Operational Training Unit — OTU, which is the last training you do before you go to a squadron. We had not dropped any bombs before, so one warm evening they loaded us up with practice bombs and we headed south to a place near the UK south coast. We took off with a full bomb load and slowly climbed up to about seven thousand feet, approaching the coast going out towards France.

Heading towards France, the right hand engine suddenly just folded up, we could not stop it because the plane was not fitted with feathering propellers. As the plane had lost one engine, we had to think about where we were going to go down. The nearest place we could find for a successful landing was called Keevil, an American base in S.E. England.

At Keevil, as we were all Sergeants, we entered the Sergeants' mess with the Yanks, and they fired questions at us – we got along famously. The American Air Force personnel made us very welcome during our enforced stay.

I will always remember the laid-back (perhaps for our benefit) Sergeant, directing a large truck laden with canned food backing up to a shed with a brick end wall and loading bay. He yelled to the driver "Back her up Jack." The driver, probably due to inexperience, revved the motor, anxious to carry out the sergeant's wishes, he let out the clutch, and the truck took off at speed, backwards, knocking down the brick wall and part of the hut, against which up to this time the laid-back Sergeant had been leaning. We left to hide our amusement at what really was something out of a Max Sennett slapstick movie.

TOUGHENING UP COURSE AT WHITLEY BAY, SHEFFIELD, NORTH EAST ENGLAND 1943.

After finishing Operational Training on Wellington Bombers, we found out that the older planes had been taken off operations and it would be necessary for the crews to be converted to four-engine Stirling Bombers. There was a great shortage of Stirlings for training purposes, so a stint at the RAF seaside town of Whitley Bay and its Physical Training course to keep us occupied and do us some good was organised.

On our second night there, the Luftwaffe sent some JU 88's on a low-level attack. We were very impressed and went outside at night to see the attack. The anti-aircraft fire all around soon sent us inside as the shrapnel was falling everywhere. The noise of the bombs, the searchlights, and the anti-aircraft guns left a lasting impression. They did not mention that it was almost a nightly affair. As was so often the case during wartime, the soldiers were never informed of their surroundings. We soon found out there was a British submarine, based at Whitely Bay just a few hours east, which was the reason for the nightly attacks. The planes used to come in very low; so low you could see the pilots in their seats. They would turn the lights up in the cockpits so they could concentrate on what they were doing. The backlighting of the instruments would reflect on their faces. It became apparent we were in a very personal war.

The only other time I saw that sort of thing going on, the Luftwaffe sent a few night intruder bombers and they dropped some bombs onto our squadrons. One landed in the Commanding Officer's little garden which we used to raid every now and again as he liked to grow his own tomatoes. A couple of Kiwis and I, would go out and rob the garden. Although I couldn't complain about the food at Whitley Bay as it was in their interest to have crews that were fit. Admittedly, most of the meats were offal – it was awful! Brains, and that sort of thing. The French love it! My grandmother used to cook up tripe occasionally during the depression; the poor women had to do something to fill the stomachs of everyone, particularly with meat.

One day, an RAAF senior officer showed up to address us at Whitley Bay in an attempt to allay our concern for the safety of Australia as news filtered through about the bombing of Darwin and advances by the Japanese. He pointed out that there were no planes for us to fly against the Japanese and that our training would be of greater use in the overall fight against the Axis powers by keeping up the war effort against Germany.

They did not deny there was a danger from the Japanese. He pointed out that at home, we did not have the equipment they had in the UK, and that 'You've got planes you can fly here and you're wanted here', and who would not want to be wanted? Otherwise, it would be all that time wasted. They certainly made it very obvious that we would be far better off to the War effort if we stayed doing what we could do best. I think it's a natural thing for people wanting to go and defend their home. Perhaps fellows at that time, who were actually dropping bombs over Germany, might have seen it as a way of avoiding the carnage that was going on, particularly in Germany, but we were unaware of the losses. How little we knew; they kept you in the dark about everything. You did not even know what the squadron had planned.

7 Squadron with the Stirling Bomber. I was flying this type of aircraft the night I was recommended for my DFC

STIRLING CONVERSION UNIT, STRADISHALL, AUGUST 1943

We proceeded to Stradishall Conversion Unit, adjoining the fen country (swamps drained by canals), where my crew and I converted to Stirling bombers. These were stable to fly compared with the Wimpey. Being the land version of the flying boat, the plane was heavy and suffered badly from insufficient power to climb, particularly in summer. On bombing operations to the Ruhr, in the western part of Germany, on warm nights we would be lucky to reach 8,000 feet – 9,000 feet over the target. This was within 20mm cannon range from the ground and they would hosepipe it up at us, using tracer shells. The slower the hose stream appeared, the closer the shells were coming our way.

I well remember my first solo flight in the Stirling with full crew aboard, now seven with the addition of a five-foot Flight Engineer, Tom Jones and a Mid Upper Turret Gunner, Ron Wynne. Climbing out after take-off, the right outer engine failed so I did an extra circuit or two to sort it out. Finally, touchdown and rollout were okay and then I saw that a large crowd had assembled, including the Commanding Officer, Wing Commander Cox. The concern was due to the Stirling's weak undercarriage during any sideways ground swing. It broke very easily. Few Stirlings survived more than forty operational sorties due to this fault and of course, due to enemy action.

BANDIT IN THE CIRCUIT

On one of our last exercises, I was flying behind my friend Ken Gilkes. Suddenly my Mid Upper Gunner called, 'Focke-Wulf 190 passing close overhead!' Almost immediately, the FW 190 commenced firing at Ken's Stirling. I could see the tracers hitting the plane, which caught fire and crashed. With lights out, we continued our approach and landing. We later found out that Ken, thrown out of the cockpit unconscious, landed in a pool of petrol, which caught fire.

Up until that point, Ken and I had been on identical paths in our careers. We met in Sydney at Bradfield Park waiting to embark overseas. After witnessing the Japanese attack on Sydney Harbour, we endured the 'primitive' conditions of the troop trains, employed to take us to Brisbane. From there we sailed together on the 'Tasker H Bliss'; eventually landing in Canada for training. We both then went to Bournemouth, where we waited to go on Spitfires. After excelling at the night vision tests, we applied to be night fighters. Then it was off to a twin-engine conversion on Oxford aeroplanes, then both to Wellington bombers for operation training where we each selected a crew. At Stradishall — the Stirling Conversion Unit — we had adjoining houses in what used to be the married quarters. The exercise we were returning from was to be our last before joining a squadron.

Ken was terribly burned. My crew and I visited him in hospital two days later. Two of my crew fainted when they saw him suspended in a bath with saline sprays covering him. His nose, eyelids, and parts of his fingers were gone. His skin charred black on the body, arms, and lower legs. I made a point to visit him when possible. Ken lived through the crash and the frightful burns he received. He was a patient of the great Dr. Macindoe and I believe is considered to be the worst burned Australian airman to survive. Two weeks after the accident, he was telling everyone he was 'much relieved to have new eyelids'. What a rotten time he had, dozens of operations under the care of Dr. Macindoe.

In the mid 1950's I was fortunate to be in Rome, flying a Constellation with Qantas, when Ken passed through, staying overnight in Rome, on his way to London to attend a reunion of Dr Macindoe's patients and happily much of his scarring had faded.

Some time ago now Ken and I had lunch at state parliament house, for one of our Bomber Command 'get-togethers'. At that time, he had just recovered from a broken leg playing golf. He took one step back to sight a putt and fell into a deep bunker. He led a very active life until his passing in November, 2014 at the age of 91.

STIRLINGS 622 SQUADRON (3 GROUP) MILDENHALL SEPTEMBER 1943.

We fittingly commenced our operations at 622 Squadron – 3 Group, located at Mildenhall, where the Centenary Air Race to Australia began in 1936.

Mildenhall — with its showpiece Officers' Mess and ivy-covered walls — was a main base for major engineering and servicing for at least five Squadrons of Stirlings in the surrounding area.

I started bombing operations, based from there, flying Stirling four-engined aircraft. By September 1943 my crew and I had completed nine operations on the Stirlings, the last being to Berlin after which they were replaced by Lancasters as the losses were very heavy, taking into account its bomb carrying capability compared to the Lancaster.

New aircraft came in from the manufacturer, flown by Air Transport Auxiliary crews. I believe there was only one female pilot certified to fly Stirlings, and she, and her five-foot tall female Flight Engineer, would almost always deliver them. They would then fly aircraft needing major overhaul back to the factory. Quite a fuss was made of these two during lunch in the mess. It was a selection requirement for a Stirling Flight Engineer to be small, as they had to clamber through small spaces in the main spar and tail spar to check the tail wheel down-locks. This operation took some time but then, so did the landing gear operation – just under a minute to retract – all done with electric motors, no hydraulics.

Our first operation in a Lancaster was to Berlin again. We completed a further three operations when, in November, we were invited to join the Path Finder Force. By mutual agreement, we joined so that we could all stick together, as we had some testing times on the Stirlings in particular. In November, 1943, after a short course at PFF, we began operations at 7 Squadron, Oakington, near Cambridge, where we completed fifty-one ops; three of these as Master Bomber and fourteen as deputy MB, making a total of sixty-four operations.

After the war, when I was flying Lockheed Constellations through Cairo in 1949, I saw many Stirlings flown from the Military Airfield, close to the civil airfield at El Marza. Presented to the Egyptian Air Force by the UK, I was also told that the only female ATA pilot to fly Stirlings during the war (mentioned earlier), had carried out the pilot conversions. Within two years, the Egyptians had lost the lot. The same fate befell the gift of Spitfires. Under King Farouk's rule, Egypt lacked stability and purpose.

STIRLING OPERATIONS SEPTEMBER 1943

I have selected from my sixty-four raids over Europe, most of which were at night, some of the most memorable missions from which we were lucky to survive. A Tour of Duty in Bomber Command was thirty operations. Ours extended to 64 operations.

For the most part the RAF conducted the night raids and the US Air Force the day raids. On 15th September 1943, our first operation was to Mt Luçon in Southern France – there was brilliant moonlight, with an excellent view of the Alps. The force of the bomb blasts bounced off the mountains sending shockwaves that we could feel through our plane. Our flight time for this was six hours, at night.

On 22nd September 1943, we had an engine failure half an hour short of the target in Hanover, Germany. We turned back with subsequent loss of altitude and speed, becoming an isolated aircraft over enemy territory.

On 27th September 1943, again to Hanover, losses were heavy – 9% of the Stirlings did not return. This could be due to the low altitude reached by the Stirlings and cannon fire from the ground. We bombed from only 9,000 feet. We had a fuel tank holed with rapid fuel loss and were lucky to make it home. It was touch and go to get back across France and the Channel. We radioed ahead, and they lit up Tangmere on the south coast and we scraped in with little fuel to spare. 111 Stirlings were on this raid – 10 were lost – 9% loss. Our flight time for this was five hours and thirty-five minutes, at night.

MINE LAYING IN THE BALTIC OCTOBER 1943

On the night of 2nd October 1943, we set out on our second mine laying trip (codenamed 'Gardening'), loaded with a new type of mine, which had to be triggered by a Naval Officer specialist assigned to fly with us. This was a single aircraft operation and we kept low over the North Sea and very low over Denmark. We flew south down the Kattegat, then East to the Baltic Sea and carried out our drop.

It was a bright moonlit night and we were flying low across Denmark, which was a great place to fly, the tallest buildings were three storeys and there was no high ground. Of course, when you get into fjord country it is a different story. As we were en route, we made out the vague shape of an aircraft, we were unable to define anything that we could recognise, but we did not think it was one of ours. So we decided to go around the top and not go across Denmark as we were not close enough to be able to see the markings on the plane. We were just being safe. On dark nights you would not see other planes, but we were constantly under surveillance. We had two little lights in the cockpit that received radio signals from the ground. When a plane crossed underneath us, the radio signal would be broken and the little lights would come on. The survival instinct takes over in that situation.

It was so very difficult to see out of the planes, no matter how hard you looked out, and you just could not see anything. My rear gunners cut the Perspex out of part of the windows, to get a clear view.

We had found the Germans had worked out the best position to target was the port side, between the two engines on the left. There were a lot of fuel lines gathered there and it was a good place to do a lot of damage. Prior to that they used to try and get right underneath and shoot the bomb carriages. They would hit the bombs and the bombs would explode in the plane. They lost a few night fighters that way.

Our main defence against that kind of attack was to wind in as much bank as you could and try to slide down or go up and be a moving target and try and lose the night fighter, particularly if he's underneath you. The night fighters trained to shoot and get out of there, always tried to remain hidden from view. There were so many bombers that we did not know how they were being shot down. We did not know until after the war that the Germans called the whole routine of the night fighter, being in position under the wing, Shräge Musik, meaning Big Sound or War Thunder!

We knew about some of their technologies. They had quite a number of different planes, but we never had any training in the

German planes. The day we were sent to the 7 Squadron, there were blokes testing a few planes and there was lots of movement going on. We still had not seen one that had been flying the night before, and then we pulled up near the headquarters and there was a Stirling; it looked as though it had copped cannon fire on the back of the plane. Night fighters were all equipped with cannons. Cannon fire was much more fatal to a plane than gunfire. The bullets used for those were fairly large 303 bullets and they had a lead case at the front. We would have loved to have a cannon. Eventually we received them towards the end of the war. Our rear gunner had four Browning machine guns and when he touched the trigger, lashings of lead would go. They used .5 shells that acted like a cannon. The cannons did a marvellous job getting air superiority from the daytime raids. They had much more effect, but you needed good lighting to be able to see your target to make use of the extra range of the cannon. I think for protection, I would rather have seen us with many more bullets, but it was most effective.

MANNHEIM – LUDWIGSHAFEN NOVEMBER 1943

Our eighth operation was to a well-defended target, Mannheim – Ludwigshafen on 18th November 1943. This was a diversionary raid by 114 Stirlings of which 9 were lost (8%). The main force target was Berlin. The operation to the target was normal but we encountered heavy fire, by both night fighters and flak, towards the end of the bombing run. Our No 1 engine was out due to enemy action with the usual loss of height on three engines, with more flak on the way home. The tanks had been hit, causing fuel loss and as we got closer to England, we requested an emergency landing. The nearest field was West Malling, a famous Battle of Britain airfield south of London. The flare path was lit, and we were able to fly straight in with a second engine failing through lack of fuel just before touchdown – there were plenty of holes in the wings and fuselage! The Spitfire pilots based at West Malling were very helpful the next day and envied our very active part in the war. Their job at that time was boring with little or no action – not like the Battle of Britain days.

As the plane was going to take a long time to repair, the crew and I received some cash and we were told to find our own way back to Mildenhall by train, via London. The only clothes we had were what we stood in — our flying boots, heavy roll-neck white pullovers, and flying jackets. We received many curious looks on the train and walking in London. The Military Police questioned us many times, thinking we might have been German Airmen or U-Boat crew.

STIRLING TO BERLIN NOVEMBER 1943

Berlin had a reputation because naturally the German people were sick and tired of the planes coming over and dropping bombs, so Hitler did everything possible to get every gun firing. They had searchlights galore and a very good radar, which was bad luck for us.

Our luckiest trip on 22nd November 1943 was to be our last on the Stirlings. Of the fifty Stirlings dispatched on this mission, five planes were lost and Bomber Command decided that Stirlings were finished as bombers.

At briefing, they advised that there would be some cloud in the target area. We found cloudy conditions at around 12,000 ft on the way to the target, and due to strong tail winds, we arrived a little early. Berlin itself was clear and we dropped our bombs. Before the bomb doors had closed, our right inboard engine received a hit and burst into flames. By cutting the fuel and stopping the propeller, we were able to put the fire out, then, turned for the long, slow flight home. The aircraft, of course, lost height and stabilised at around 6,000 ft.

We then entered heavy cloud and freezing rain causing clear ice to form. I could see it building up on the stationary propeller and over the wings, adding tons of weight to the aircraft. The crew threw everything moveable overboard – all of the ammunition, all guns. We had our chutes on and ready, as the plane sank to 3,000 ft, still in heavy cloud. All this time the navigation had been on dead reckoning – Dave, the navigator, thought we must be nearing the Dutch coast. We were near to 1500 ft in cloud, the ice starting to melt, when the cloud all around lit up and anti-aircraft shells burst loudly above the engine noise. The cordite smell was very strong. The ice melted once we reached the sea and we high-tailed it for home. They were about to give us up as missing because the return trip had been so slow. The round trip had taken seven hours, all night and hand flown.

The Lancaster

LANCASTERS NOVEMBER 1943

After the bombing raids, we were to train for low-level night flights over France for drops to the French Resistance. The Stirling was well suited for this task, the sleeve valve engines being rather quiet, and the plane very longitudinally stable. Daily we would fly low over the fen country and up to the Wash past Norwich. This low flying was a pilot's dream come true. We were about to start low flying on moonlight nights when our Squadron was supplied with Lancaster Bombers. After a rapid conversion at Mildenhall, we flew our first Lancaster. The operation was to Berlin on the night of 31st January

1944. Losses were heavy – 32 lost from a force of 440 (7.2%) Our flight time was six hours and twenty-five minutes, at night.

STUTTGART, FEBRUARY 1944

Over Germany on 20th February 1944, our main entrance door lock broke and the door opened. Stan Williamson, the Wireless Operator, used some parachute cord and tied it firmly closed. On return to Mildenhall, at dispersal, they opened the bomb doors after stopping all engines. This was to allow the ground crew to check that there were no bombs held up in the racks. Unfortunately, two incendiaries dropped onto the tarmac below the plane and burst into flames. There was a scramble to exit the plane through the main door, which took a little time to open due to Stan's 'granny' knots. The ground crew was quick to push our plane away from the fires.

NUREMBERG

From the 30th – 31st March 1944 we saw the heaviest loss of any raid. The 95 aircraft comprised of 655 crewmembers and equivalent to 12% of the inbound force from the Belgian border to the target. In one hour, 82 aircraft were shot down. In that short time, 572 aircrew were lost and a further 16 aircraft were lost on the return flight to UK, bringing the total to 98 lost planes. We missed this raid as we were at the Pathfinder's school at Warboys, learning marking techniques.

As mentioned before, we became known in the squadron as 'The Lucky Crew'. None of us missed a trip, which was unusual. Steve Harper, the latest crew addition had many more operations to complete his quota. He copped some shrapnel in the chest on the second op. he did after leaving us, and wound up in hospital. Every one of my crew received a DFC and a promotion to officer rank on completion of the double tour. The rear gunner, John Naylor wanted to go back to his old job as a gardener on a large estate and said he wanted to remain an NCO and was therefore awarded a DFM.

ROYAL AIR FORCE

PATH FINDER FORCE

Award of Path Finder Force Badge

This is to certify that

FLIGHT LIEUTENANT F. A. PHILLIPS.
AUS. 409939

having qualified for the award of the Path Finder Force Badge, and having now completed satisfactorily the requisite conditions of operational duty in the Path Finder Force, is hereby

Permanently awarded the Path Finder Force Badge

Issued this **10th** day of **SEPTEMBER** in the year 19**44**

Air Officer Commanding, Path Finder Force.

Path Finder Force

WARBOYS, PATHFINDER FORCE MARCH 1944

During 1942, night bombing over Europe was very inaccurate; because of this an Australian Wing Commander — DCT Bennett — introduced the Pathfinder Force; an elite group of volunteers selected by invitation. The latest aids to navigation enabled them to find and mark targets with brightly coloured flares. A Master Bomber then gave precise instructions to the main bomber force, directing the attack.

On 3rd March 1944, we received advice that we had been selected to join the Path Finder Force. We did a short course at their training airfield, Warboys, practicing precision bombing and studying the PFF methods of target marking.

One of the reasons for our elevation to the Pathfinder Force was the high standard of navigation from our navigator, Dave Goodwin (RNZAF). After our second trip with PFF, he was selected to radio back the wind velocity he found at altitude (code-named 'Zephyring'), as we would be some minutes ahead of the main bomber force. This meant breaking radio silence — the Wireless Operator sent the found wind velocity by Morse code to the following listening main force.

NO. 7 SQUADRON (8 GROUP) PATHFINDER FORCE APRIL 1944

Enemy night fighters were continually trying to out-guess us with what was going to be the target and we would try and confuse them as much as possible, by making turns in our planes. A large number of planes would go round and we would drop a few markers on route. Some of the best navigators would be assigned to put down a special flare that was slow moving, and you were designated to go round it and you would go out on a certain heading, then turn and come down on the selected bombing run.

Based at Oakington, near Cambridge, No. 7 Squadron had the highest loss rate of any Squadron in the PFF and the third highest loss rate of any Squadron in Bomber Command. I can recall very few crews finishing in the normal way — the normal way meaning surviving to achieve the required number of trips. We had to do thirty trips to get to the break, and the break was at a training school to teach other pilots to fly a plane. I was never selected to teach the other pilots. They were getting too much use out of me. If you signed up for pathfinders, you had to do fifty trips, which enables you to wear a little metal wing. You had to get the trips in first, before they gave it to you.

A contributing factor to the high losses was the amount of time that Master Bomber, and Deputy Master Bomber, spent in the target area controlling the raid. If it was a long, large raid, it could mean up to twenty minutes circling the target. The instructions by radio from the Master Bomber to the main bomber force could be used by the German direction finding equipment to 'home' in night fighters.

Searchlights coned our aircraft on a number of occasions with resultant heavy flak concentration, or if no flak, it could mean enemy night fighter activity. On these raids we used Visual Re-centres — aircraft that dropped special coloured target indicators to correct the aiming point of the target. The Master Bomber could request additional marking runs by these aircraft, or request his Deputy to re-mark.

On the 19th-20th May 1944, during a night raid to Le Mans railway yards, Wing Commander Barron, DSO, DFC and DFM (RNZAF), was carrying out Master Bomber duties from our No 7 Squadron. History has presumed that W/Cdr Barron collided with his Deputy Master Bomber, resulting in the total loss of both crews. I have never accepted that explanation. I remember clearly that as we ran up to the target I came out from behind my curtain and almost the first thing that I saw was a combat slightly ahead and above us out on our starboard side. First, there were the few large and white balls of a German night fighter's cannon and then the thin red lines of .303 tracers from a rear gunner in reply. Very soon, there were sparks as the cannon shells started to hit. At the same time, the Master Bomber had just started his broadcast. His call sign that night was 'Little John', and I heard, 'Little John to Main Force, bomb the centre…' and at this time his transmission cut out. I then saw an awesome sight, which I will never ever forget. The Lancaster started to burn from nose to tail and from wingtip to wingtip with short flames as if the plane was a spectre. It rose up, and the port wing dropped and it passed above and ahead of us before spiralling down our port side. I saw no parachutes.

Quickly there came over the R/T 'Little John 2 to Little John' (pause) 'Little John 2 to Little John' as the deputy Master Bomber tried to contact W/Cdr Barron. Then came 'Little John 2 to Main Force taking over. Bomb….'; and then he, too, cut. Just at that moment in the same direction as the previous combat, I saw German cannon fire firing up at an acute angle and immediately the cannon shells hit. In the dim light of a fire starting, I thought I saw an FW190 standing almost on its tail as it hose-piped the belly of the Lancaster. Did I see two combats in which first the Master Bomber and then his deputy perished? I have always thought so. This engagement was previously reported as a collision, but new evidence is now to hand discounting this and confirms that both Master and Deputy were shot down shortly after each other over a target, as witnessed by Frank Clear, navigator with No 115 Squadron prior to joining 7 Squadron. There were no survivors.

I refer here to a publication 'No. 7 Bomber Squadron' by Tom Docherty from page 179; I quote from Alan Craig's passage:

'The Prime Minister, Winston Churchill required that part of the bomber force departing in a bombing raid to German, fly at 2000 feet over the House of Commons London at exactly 7pm. All the barrage balloons were taken down and the Air Defences notified.

As he spoke the words, 'As I speak, our Air Force is taking the war to the enemy'. The roar of many bombers must have impressed the House Members – a great showman, Winston Churchill. Our plane was one of those taking part in this exercise'.

My friend, Squadron Leader Brian Frow, DSO and DFC, RAF took over Frazer Barron's role as Master Bomber and I was his Deputy on eight operations. Returning from one raid — homeward bound over France — Brian Frow's gunners shot down three German night fighters who had attacked them. This added to an already incredible early war experience, when he damaged the stern of the Sharnhorst battleship, in a fjord, by dropping a mine from a twin-engine Hamden bomber.

The greatest number of planes that we controlled in a single raid was 1,250. The most difficult thing to acquire with all those losses was experience and 'know how'. The great urge of crews was to get out of the target area as quickly as possible. Hence the trend to press the bomb release button early. One always felt like a 'sitting duck' for those two minutes of straight and level flight.

Brian Frow finished with 75 operations. I carried out Master Bomber duties on three separate operations and I was still only 20 years old. After Brian finished, I did a further six as Deputy Master Bomber to Squadron Leader Alan Craig DSO, AFC. I finished operations a month after turning twenty-one; Brian Frow was only nine months older than I was. In total, I carried out three Master Bomber raids and fourteen Deputy Master Bomber raids. I re-made contact with Frank Shaw, who was the Officer-in-Charge of the electrical side of the aircraft – instruments and bomb loading, at 7 Squadron at Oakington. Previous to the war, we had lived a few doors from each other in Armadale, a suburb of Melbourne. I was twelve years old when we first met. One evening as we were leaving the airfield on pushbikes, a Mosquito twin-engined bomber had undercarriage trouble on take-off. The gear collapsed, the plane slithered on its belly not far from us and we threw ourselves on the ground as this small plane had one huge 4,000lb (two Tonne) bomb in its belly. Fortunately, it did not go off. Frank and I have remained close friends to this day.

PFF aircraft were the first to be fitted with H2S Radar, a useful navigation device displaying ground features (rivers, lakes, coastlines, and large towns). We were not aware until after the war that the Germans had one of these sets from a crashed Stirling very soon after its introduction. The self destruct explosive charge in the new equipment failed to operate and the Germans were quick to assess the radar frequency and used it to accentuate the radar blip return, thus increasing the range of both the giant Wurlitzer used by the fighter controller and the little Wurlitzer radar carried on their night fighters. Within one month they had a device fitted to their radars, which used the H2S transmitted signal to 'home' in their night fighters. This accounted for a large number of bomber losses. We only became aware of this fact after we finished operations. The practice, later, was to use the equipment (H2S) as little as possible.

It is amazing and frightening to think about the amount of hidden details that emerge after a war. For instance, some of the JU88 night fighters had a 60° forward sloping, almost vertically fixed cannon mounted. This enabled the fighter to get under our blind spot and then blow the plane out of the sky with explosive shells. No-one came back to tell about this device. It was 100% effective. There is a most illuminating book called 'The Most Secret War', written by one of the 'boffins', that details some of these things I have mentioned.

The German raids on London were very accurate as they used radio beams from stations, located near the northern coast of France, from Normandy around to Calais. Their bombers had comparatively short distances to travel over hostile territory. After the invasion of Europe, allied beam stations were installed in France and later Belgium, allowing high-speed mosquito aircraft to accurately mark the targets. This was code-named 'oboe'. It was then our job to be there, exactly on time, and to keep the spot continuously marked during the raid, and this could last for ten to twenty minutes. Prior to that time, it was necessary to rely on dropping illuminating flares, and hope that our specialist map readers/bomb aimers could identify some salient feature and mark that point.

No. 7 Squadron had two visits from the Royal Family. HM King George VI invested me with the DFC on his second visit in 1944. After the investiture, afternoon tea was served in the Mess for the Royal Family, including the then Princess Elizabeth, and for those who received decorations that day. The Queen happened to see all the other Officers having their tea in the billiard room as arranged by our Commodore, however, she insisted that we all come to the Mess and have afternoon tea with the Royal Family. The Queen was not too pleased with our Air Commodore, poor chap! At about this time, I was awarded a Bar to my DFC. The actual Bar arrived by mail after I returned to Australia. The reason for its late arrival was the fact that in the meantime, I had flown home across the Pacific and was operating against Japan.

KARLSRUHE PATHFINDER FORCE APRIL 1944

Over Germany, on the way to the target on 24th April 1944, the electric heating of the pitot tubes failed, causing ice to block the tubes. Airspeed indications ceased and static air for the altimeter gave erroneous readings. We proceeded to the target and just after we had dropped our bombs, flak hit our port inner engine. We lost all the oil and feathered (stopped) the engine before it seized. We headed home in cloud, losing altitude and speed. With our vital instruments missing, Dave, my Navigator, was having great difficulty with dead reckoning as we were in cloud. We strayed over what must have been Strasbourg where we encountered heavy anti-aircraft fire – intense noise and giant flashes of light from exploding anti-aircraft shells lit up the cloud with the occasional sound of shrapnel hitting the plane. What a charmed life – not one of our crew was hit! Instrument indications returned to normal before we got to the coast of England when the ice melted as we began to descend into warmer air. Our flying time for that mission was six hours.

At this time I was allotted an extra crewmember, Warrant Officer A J Harper, RAF, as a specialist Map Reader and Bomb Aimer. Clive Thurston became Radar Operator and Navigator 2 to Dave Goodwin. This made a total crew of eight.

During these raids we had close bursts of flak; one could hear over the engine noise some of the small pieces of shrapnel hitting the plane like hail. The smell of burnt cordite was very strong. My Flight Engineer, Tom Jones, in his memoirs said he counted eighty-five holes starting at the tail and got as far as the mid upper gun turret then stopped counting. He also made a point to remind me we were called 'The Lucky Crew' as we had all completed the sixty-four trips together without a scratch. The one place where all bomber crews wanted to be away from was the target area. As soon as the bombs had gone and the bomb doors closed they would speed up and get out of there as quickly as possible. My crew did seventeen trips where we would remain in the target area, ensuring the aiming point was kept marked throughout the raid and making another run if necessary, or if asked to by the Master.

As Deputy on fourteen of these raids, the Master and I would converse by VHF on an agreed private frequency as to what correction to the aiming point may be necessary. We could be over the target for up to twenty minutes on a long raid. Timing was all-important. The Mosquito fitted with OBOE (code name for the electronic beams) would drop his target indicator and we would have to re-mark it rapidly, as it had a short life. I was assigned a specialist bomb aimer/map-reader over my last twenty flights. My regular Bomb aimer became 2nd Navigator assisting with radar fixes as Dave, my navigator, passed his found winds (wind at altitude) back to the main force following. Radio silence was broken for the transmission of 'Zephyring'. Searchlights coned our plane on a number of occasions as we circled the target for a considerable time. My mid-upper Gunner, Ron Wynne is the only other member still alive today.

I did two more trips as Master Bomber, one on the 4th July 1944, and one on the 28th August 1944, both on Flying Bomb sites. Heavy and accurate flak was encountered on the latter raid, which was to Oeuf en Ternois.

D-DAY, JUNE 5TH 1944

I was selected to lead about 200-300 planes to knock out three big marine naval guns that were positioned, just in from Cannes. When we got over the target, we could not see anything; we were in a thick sea fog so all I could do was drop on "GEE" (Generalised Estimating Equation, navigation system). As far as my job was concerned, I could do no more than that. I was a Master Bomber and it was found that our boss, T C B Bennet, reckoned it was far better for one man to be in charge, because if it's more than one man, to be dependent on others, confuses the processes.

We knew it was D-day, because when we turned back, the radar showed up hundreds and hundreds of vessels and war ships firing away and everything was 'go go go'. This was something we had waited for, for a long time, and we still cannot believe it was carried out so well. It was terribly well done. It was not so much the secrecy, but the fooling of the Germans, they had planned all kinds of things further up the coast in Calais — spoof signals — we made them think we were definitely going further up the coast. Getting that first foothold was the important thing.

We had planned to get to the target three minutes before the attack was due to start. In three minutes, the Master Bomber would have to sort out the markers and work out if the bombs were being dropped onto the correct target, because there was no way they could refresh their memory once they had seen that the markers had gone down — these were dropped by Pathfinders' flying mosquitoes. If my men thought that the bomber was getting away from the original marked area, we would have to go in and re-mark with a different coloured flare. We could also change the height of the bomb release.

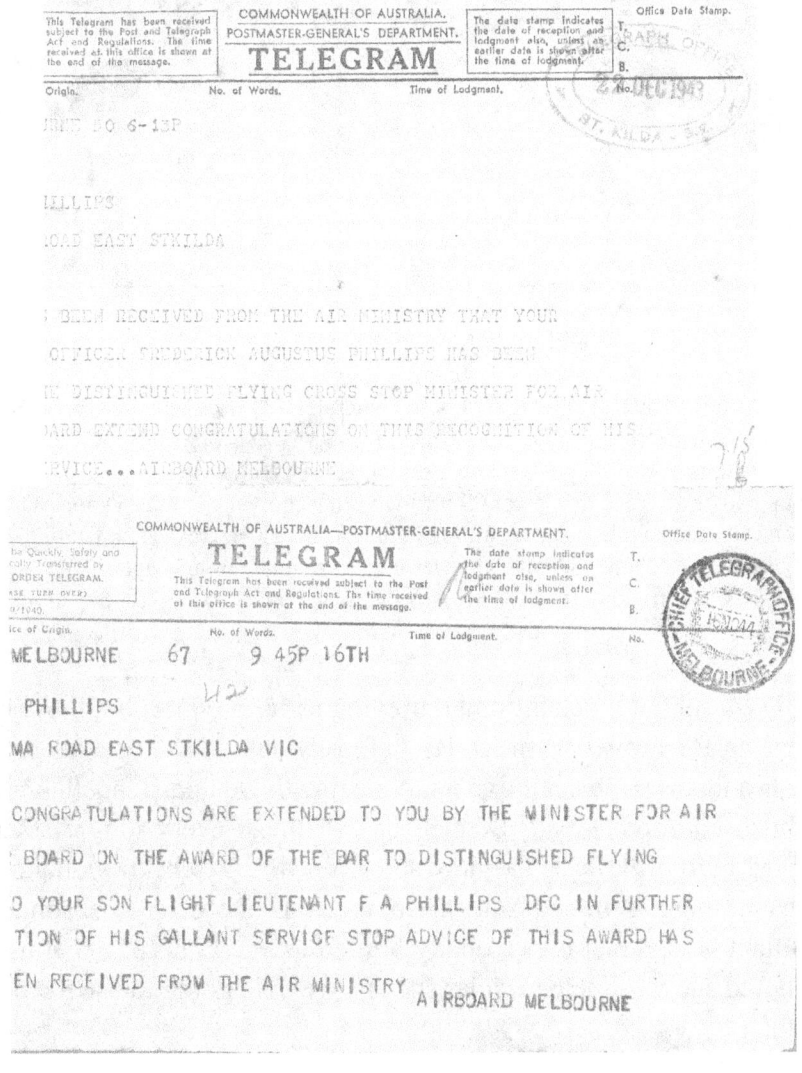

Telegram re: DFC Award

DFC Investiture by Kind George VI.
In this photo :
Self: Decorated by King George V1, also pictured, HRH Elizabeth the Queen, HRH Princess Elizabeth, (now Queen Elizabeth 11) Air Vice Marshall DCT Bennett, WAAF Squadron Officer, Daphne Pearson GC (George Cross) One of only 3 women to be awarded this decoration which is the equivalent of the Victoria Cross, Daphne rescued a pilot from a burning fighter plane which crashed on landing. She emigrated to Adelaide, SA after the war. Extreme right, Group Captain Townsend, the Kings equerry and at this time, was the man Princess Margaret hoped to one day marry.

They did not muck around retrieving us for the mission; they sent a car up for Frow and me a day before D-day. They took us out to the headquarters for Pathfinders to meet with Donald Bennett, a man I much admired. Donald Bennett broke almost every long distance record before the war. He flew solo from Prestwick in Scotland to Johannesburg, setting up all the navigation himself — absolutely brilliant navigator. He personally briefed us. At night they sent us to Fellet to show us the particular shells they were going to use the next night.

On the night of the mission we bombed from about four thousand feet. When we returned to the base, there was Monty (Montgomery, the general in charge). He gathered the troops and told us the whole thing had been a great success, and thanked us for a job well done.

FLYING BOMB SITE OISEMONT PATHFINDER FORCE, JUNE 1944

My first Master Bomber trip was a daylight attack on a Flying Bomb site on 30th June 1944, at Oisemont with 107 aircraft. Flight Lieutenant 'Nobby' Clarke from our No 7 Squadron had been shot down the day before, carrying out the Master Bomber role. He survived the war as a POW.

CAEN, PATHFINDER FORCE, JULY 1944

Our job on this raid was to visually re-centre the markers with specially coloured target indicators in the Normandy battle area, east of Caen, from a height of 5,000 feet. As the trip was short and at low altitude, I decided to proceed on three engines from Reading, west of London, outbound, after one of our inboard engines failed. Our flight time for this was three hours and fifteen minutes, by day.

HOMBERG PATHFINDER FORCE, JULY 1944

We were visually re-centring on this raid to Homberg on the 20 – 21st July, 1944, which meant two or three runs over the target to re-mark the aiming point visually. There were enemy night fighters in large numbers and my gunners had a busy night. We saw aircraft falling, on fire, at 14,000 feet. We experienced very heavy losses —20 of 147 Lancasters, 13.6% loss. No 75 Squadron RNZAF lost 7 of the 25 Lancasters they dispatched on this raid. Our flight time was three hours and twenty minutes, by night.

NORMANDY BATTLE AREA - PATHFINDER FORCE, AUGUST 1944

During early August 1944, the strongest German resistance was occurring against the British forces around Caen. General Montgomery requested bomber assistance. Squadron Leader Brian Frow and I were taken to Group Headquarters at Newmarket where we were briefed by Air Vice Marshal Bennett (our boss of Pathfinders) to proceed on the following night, 6th August 1944, over the battle area to observe some special artillery shells which would indicate our aiming point for a subsequent raid.

On the following night, 7th August 1944, saw 1,019 aircraft dispatched. The targets were German ground troops opposing the advance by the Allied Army. The raid report read as 'carefully controlled and successful'. Ten Lancasters were lost. Brian was Master Bomber and I was his Deputy, controlling this vital raid.

Another similar raid followed on the night of 12th August 1944, with 144 aircraft against enemy troop concentrations at the Falaise Gap, to prevent the escape of a large enemy force. I was Deputy Master Bomber again on this raid, which was reported as 'very effective'. Two days later I celebrated my twenty-first birthday in Bournemouth.

On my twenty-first birthday I came back from a trip and Frank Shaw, a flight lieutenant mate of mine, was in charge of all the photography, the loading of the bombs and all the flight instruments. He was a professional photographer and he took many pictures of us. Thanks to Frank I have some fine photographs from those days. The day Frank arrived to work with our Squadron was also the day the King awarded me with the DFC. Frank saw the parade and the crowd and drove right in. He almost interrupted the King pinning on my DFC!

As for entertainment, after they had us up and down sand hills and on route marches — as part of our daily routine —we were able to get into Newcastle at night and find amusement in smoke-filled pubs where there were Polish night fighter pilots, who were based nearby.

The blackout was pretty difficult during those times. You just had to open your mouth and ask people where something was and they would say, 'Oh, it's right there!'

We got talking to the Polish night fighter boys, when we could understand them; there was one particularly quick fellow, Zurozowsky and he had taken out a few German fighters, and of course that's what we wanted to do. We would have liked to be night fighter pilots, but it did not happen. There was a tremendous shortage of pilots to fly the planes.

The pub was really just a case of an interesting place to talk to people. We did not drink to get full or anything, it was just a thing that was for socialising. You could hardly see across the room due to the blackout curtains. There was absolutely no air and the place was full of smoke. Terrible. Unfortunately, in order to have any real fun, you had to know where the dances were being held. If you could get to the pub, you could find out where the dances were. Cambridge was our hunting ground for girls. I loved dancing and we did not get a great amount of exercise. Those days I used to dance at about forty miles an hour, you would whip around the dance floor. It slowed down a bit with a slow Foxtrot.

The most famous group was Joe Loss and his band. They had very good singers – including the fellow who sang 'Begin the Beguine'. All the top American bandleaders were over there, with Joe Loss considered the best English bandleader at that time. After D-Day, the first item they set up on the French side was a radio station called GI Joe. Sergeant Johnny Johnson was their announcer – very popular fellow.

COMMONWEALTH OF AUSTRALIA

.130.

97419

55/1/783.

DEPARTMENT OF AIR

NOV 21 1946

MELBOURNE, 1.

Sir,

  I desire to inform you advice has now been
received from Overseas Headquarters, R.A.A.F., to the
effect that you have been awarded the Croix de Guerre by
the French authorities in recognition of service rendered
in France or in air operations directly connected with the
liberation of France.

  This Department extends congratulations on
this recognition of your splendid service.

  Yours faithfully,

(M. C. Langslow)
<u>Secretary</u>.

A. Phillips,
te Road,
NIAL PARK, N.S.W.

STETTIN IN POLAND, NEAR THE EAST GERMAN BORDER ABOUT SIXTY KM IN FROM THE BALTIC SEA COASTLINE – PATHFINDER FORCE, AUGUST 1944

On 29th August 1944, we carried out our longest all night operation to Stettin in Poland. There was plenty of flak over the target. A total of 23 Lancasters were lost on this operation, 5.7% of the force. Our flight time was nine hours and ten minutes, at night.

Throughout WWII, only a single pilot operated each plane in Bomber Command. This was a long time to be at the controls, particularly at night. Like most pilots, I used no instrument lighting, relying only on the luminous painted dials to retain maximum night vision. The exception to this was when we were over a well-lit target or when coned by searchlights.

Just before leaving Oakington the RAF advised me that the French Government had awarded me the Croix de Guerre for outstanding war services rendered during operations for the liberation of France.

By this time I was suffering terribly with hemorrhoids; I think the absence of fruit had something to do with the rather common complaint for us colonials serving in England. Anyway, the Squadron doctor gave me a suppository for the long flight to Stettin now known as Gdansk. The affect soon wore off and I had a rather painful ten hours in the seat. The next day it was off to the Cambridge University hospital to have minor surgery. Dating a nurse from that hospital, I was petrified that she may be in attendance. Fortunately this was not the case.

I was prepared and on all fours on the operating table, shot up with local anaesthetic, when a loud voiced doctor followed by a number of medical students, male and female about my age, entered. He was very similar to James Robertson Justice who was the actor in the film, 'Dr in the House'. He said, 'I'll make an incision just here' and the next thing a spurt of blood hit my heel. There was some light laughter from the students, which he very loudly Stopped. I was back flying two nights later, much relieved.

The Lucky Crew photographed by my friend from school, Frank Shaw

STONEY CROSS, SEPTEMBER 1944

In September 1944, after finishing the sixty-four Bombing Operations, I received a posting to the new Transport Squadron, formed at Stoney Cross Airfield in the New Forest, recently vacated by the US Air Force. We were astonished when the first planes arrived – they were old Wellington 1C's with Pegasus engines, non-feathering propellers and passenger seating! I flew these during my Operational Training days, and knew that they could not hold altitude on one engine. We did some circuit flying and started training pilots who had not previously flown the Wellington, in readiness to transport troops out to East India and Burma. They scrapped the whole project when the inability to hold height on one engine was 'discovered' by the Powers-That-Be.

Stoney Cross Airfield was only a mile or two from the home of the famous Sir Arthur Conan Doyle, who wrote the Sherlock Holmes series.

Later, we moved to another ex-US Air Force base, Merryfield, in Somerset, where we converted to Dakota DC3's. This training on DC3's was in preparation for our coming role in the Pacific War Zone. There were approximately 30 crews – as I recall. Each crew had one pilot, one navigator, and one wireless operator. We proceeded north in trucks by road to Glasgow where we boarded the Queen Elizabeth for the journey to New York on approximately 10th March, 1945.

Before I leave the UK theatre of war, I will relate a few of the incidents I experienced whilst off duty during this time.

Lord Nuffield, of Morris car fame, provided free luxury hotel accommodation throughout England and Scotland to air crew from the Empire. Thanks to his generosity we spent our leave very comfortably accommodated.

It was my good fortune to receive an invitation from Lord Barnard to the wonderful Raby Castle in County Durham. The castle is close to the small town of Staindrop. I had the Blue Room. While the butler unpacked my meagre belongings, a huge bath was made ready and I was told some early King had slept in the bed I used. Lord Barnard took over as Chief Scout after Lord Baden Powell died. On the third day his son came home from Eton and he gave me the complete tour of the castle. From the battlements — where there was a huge cauldron from which molten lead could be poured down on to the drawbridge crossing the moat as a welcome to unwanted strangers — to the kitchens, secret passages, cellars, and dungeons. Lady Barnard took me to her indoor hothouse where, in pride of place was, a small Australian gum tree. The smell of Eucalyptus gave me instant nostalgia for home.

Raby Castle

Another time I was the sole passenger on the platform of an immaculately kept railway station waiting for the steam train to London. The Station Master informed me that the author HG Wells was booked into the same compartment and he introduced me to Mr Wells when he arrived. As a teenager, I had read most of Wells' books, in particular the one about a trip to the moon using anti-gravitation blinds. This very dapper, handsome man had a great personality, making the trip to London most enjoyable. His writings about the future may yet come to pass, as recently an anti-gravity device has been demonstrated, according to our newspapers.

I had some driving experience prior to WWII, driving mainly at night with a newspaper Cub Reporter in his Morris 8/40 1935 Model. When I arrived at 622 Squadron, Mildenhall, I bought a 350cc BSA motorbike for £10 ($20.00). Riding this bike at night was rather difficult because of its poor lighting. The headlight was fitted with what looked like a large jam tin with slits cut in the front, allowing very little light to penetrate through. This was a requirement for the blackout.

The longest trip I did was with my Rear Gunner John Naylor riding pillion to his home in Melton Mowbray in Leicestershire, 80 or 100 miles – as I recall. When winter arrived, I found the bike hard to keep from sliding on the icy roads so I sold it and bought a car. Someone had heard that a group of gypsies had a car they wanted to sell, so we set off on pushbikes to find their camp. It was just as portrayed in films – the horse-drawn travelling home etc. The car was a Ford 8 Tourer – with smart cut-away sporty doors and cost £30. They could not, get petrol, of course, as was the case with most civilians so they were lucky to get a buyer.

I went to the local Post Office — one lady proprietor — and paid 2/6d (25c) for a driver's licence and was on my way. However, with winter and the snow, I found the Tourer too cold and wet, so I sold it to an Air Force chap and for £20 and I bought a Ford 10 sedan, which I kept until I left England.

Later when I joined Transport Command at Stoney Cross, we found, deep in the New Forest, a huge stack of four-gallon drums of eighty-octane petrol left by the Americans. All car owners on the station had as much fuel as they could use.

Back in Australia, in 1945, I bought a 1936 Standard Chevrolet sedan when I was demobbed – a real bomb! I found it had been used throughout the war with a gas-producer on the rear of the car. Mother and I drove it from Melbourne to Sydney in early January 1946, with as much gear as it could possibly hold. We had lots of troubles on the way and it was very hot! We averaged thirty miles per hour and it took days. In 1948, I bought a brand new Standard 8 for £465($930.00). Haze and I drove it to Brisbane on our honeymoon in September 1948

DC3'S MONTREAL TO SYDNEY, 1945

The journey on the Queen Elizabeth to New York departed Greenock on 10th March 1945, and was the antithesis of my two previous ship voyages — only about twenty of us, Officers, in absolute luxury. The ship was full of badly wounded US troops from the invasion of Europe — all hospital cases. The Captain engaged me as the Aircraft Recognition Officer and I spent much time up on the bridge. I was able to accompany the Duty Officer on his rounds and saw a great deal of the ship.

After berthing at New York we proceeded to Montreal where I took delivery of a brand new Dakota DC3 for the journey to Australia. As I recall, approximately twelve DC3's were to make the journey. For the next ten days, each pilot had to complete twenty hours of Radio Range flying in Link Trainers before the US Government would allow us to fly to the west coast via the then airway system of radio beams. The route took us from Duval Airfield in Montreal to Elizabeth City in Maryland on 4th April 1945, where we stayed overnight, proceeding next day to Dallas, Texas, where we stopped for the night again. The local Texans entertained us very well as few of them had met wartime British airmen. The next day we flew, at spaced intervals again, along the El Paso Pass through the mountains to Tucson, Arizona, then to Fresno and to Mather Field at Sacramento,

California. Here we awaited favourable winds for the long ocean leg to John Rogers Field at Honolulu. This was the longest stage and took fourteen hours thirty-five minutes. We had extra fuel tanks in the main cabin made from plywood with brass steam cocks. The take-off weight I remember was 35,000lbs, compared with today's maximum of 26,500lbs for the DC3. We had six days in Honolulu and I recall Kalakau Avenue with just two hotels, the Royal Hawaiian and the Moana. The few remaining buildings were small and scattered, mostly with palm-thatched roofs. The PX (Post Exchange US Army store) had a branch at the Moana Hotel and had some surfboards for hire. I hired one that must have been fifteen foot long and so heavy I had to drag it to the water. The waves were small and the coral close to the surface. I could not manage the enormous thing. The Malibu board did not appear until almost five years later. The three of us, Flying Officer Paddy Quaine (Navigator) and Warrant Officer John Hewitt (Wireless Operator) got to know some Super Fortress crews waiting to fly out to the Pacific War theatre, leaving on the same day as ourselves. They invited us to their navigation briefing. They had organised large quantities of beer and a red-haired shapely young woman did a strip to keep everyone interested. I often wonder if her name was Mamie Stover, a local prostitute who gained later fame from her books.

We had an uneventful flight from Honolulu to Sydney, stopping overnight at Canton Island, which had only one palm tree — the highest thing on the island — then on to Nadi, Fiji, which at the time was just a grass strip. The day after, we flew to Auckland where I stayed overnight with Dave Goodwin, my New Zealand Navigator, who had returned earlier by ship. The next day we flew direct to Camden, outside Sydney; the flying time from Auckland was eight hours forty-five minutes into a very strong headwind.

DC3 DAKOTAS IN THE PACIFIC —
No 243 SQUADRON RAF CAMDEN, 1945

When I returned to Australia, after a brief leave, and still seconded to the RAF, I flew Dakota DC3's out of Camden to supply the Royal Navy in the Pacific. We would load up at Mascot then on to Brisbane; Townsville; Milne Bay in New Guinea then north to Momote Airfield on Los Negros Island, which served Manus Island.

As the Americans advanced westward across the various islands, my flights up north kept increasing in distance. The next stop was the Palau Islands, east of the Philippines. The airfield was on Peleliu Island. We arrived there on 21st June 1945. The largest island in the group is Babelthuap, where large numbers of Japanese troops were trapped and starving. Some of them would swim across at night, during low tide, to Peleliu to pick up scraps. There was a PX in one of the very few buildings on the island – the rest was just flat, white coral. Everyone, including ourselves, slept on camp stretchers out in the open.

Approaching Peleliu one day, at 6,000 feet, Ground Control warned of 'Bandits' (enemy aircraft). There were transport planes everywhere and all of us headed for one isolated, huge cumulus cloud for safety. It is hard to believe that there were no collisions even though it was very rough flying for twenty minutes or so until the 'all clear' was given. On a side note, while in Peleliu I had the pleasure of meeting the actor, Tyrone Power, who was a US Navy pilot based there.

Next stop was Leyte Island in the Philippines where the airstrip was at Tacloban – at that time it was the busiest airfield in the world. There were huge bulldozers standing alongside the PSP (all steel runway) ready to push any plane that had a mishap off the runway to maintain a constant traffic flow.

MEDICAL EVACUATIONS FROM AITAPE, NEW GUINEA 1945

Our Dakotas could convert very easily to carry a stretcher. Whenever we carried hospital cases, an English Nursing Sister was assigned to fly with us. I cannot, for the life of me, remember her name but she was a FANY (First Aid Nursing Yeomanry). They always issued me with a revolver and ammunition to protect her, as she would often be the only female on some of the islands where we landed.

In early June 1945 we flew to Manus Island, then back to Lae, and then up the Markham Valley to Aitape (Tadji airfield). Next day, we left with a full load of patients — some stretchered and some walking. We had to fly past Wewak, still held by the Japanese, giving it a very wide berth as we did on the way up to Tadji. At Wewak there was a Japanese anti-aircraft gunner nicknamed 'Dead-Eye Dick'. He had a terrific reputation and accounted for a number of kills throughout the war.

A little later, on the same flight, the Sister asked for my assistance to stop the walking wounded throwing a Japanese POW out the rear door. My Navigator and Wireless Operator went back and found the Aussies had opened the main cargo door. My crew sorted out the situation, putting the Japanese POW in the toilet, as it was the stench of his gangrenous leg that had caused the trouble. The rest of the flight to Lae was uneventful.

1945 – VE DAY

I spent VE (Victory Europe) Day, 9th May 1945, at Momote airfield near Manus Island. We received the news when we arrived in the late afternoon, after stopping at Milne Bay on the way north from Townsville. Wonderful News! The end of the war in Europe gave us hope that the defeat of the Japanese would soon follow.

The officers' mess was located close to the runway, near the beach. My Navigator, Wireless Operator, and myself were in for a dull evening when from out of the blue a big Sky Master landed and forty-five young American girls in civilian clothing came into the mess. They were there to raise morale and carry out administration type duties. There were only three US officers off duty that night and none of the girls had ever met an Australian so it turned out to be a far from dull tropical night after all. The next day we took off for Townsville.

In July 1945, flying in from Peleliu to Tacloban Airfield on Leyte Island, my Navigator, Wireless Operator and I were given permission to fly over the largest congregation of naval vessels ever assembled in one place — two American Fleets and the Royal Navy Pacific Fleet. They were closely gathered to put up a tremendous firepower against Kamikaze attacks in the Leyte Gulf.

As the American forces advanced and occupied Luzon Island, our flights terminated at Manila. In late July, an RAF co-pilot, Sergeant Marsland, was assigned to my crew and remained with me until I finished on 28th November 1945. As I mentioned earlier, it was RAF policy to have single pilot operations, but after VE Day a surplus of pilots came about. After VJ Day we had the luxury of using landing lights at night for the first time in my flying career.

VJ DAY, 1945

On 15th August 1945, arriving back in the late afternoon at Camden Airfield from a flight to Manus Island, we found that there were crowds of people all over the airfield. I had to wait for a clearing large and safe enough to land. It was VJ (Victory Japan) Day! (I might add that it was always VJ Day. Only in recent times the term VP (Victory Pacific) has been used; I disagree with this term.

That night there were a number of barbecues out on the airfield. The Macarthur family, who owned all the land around the airfield, provided the food for this joyous occasion.

At this time, I was reminded of the years when I was a young child, living with my grandparents in Maryborough, Victoria. Our school went for a sports picnic to Bet Bet, approximately twenty miles from Maryborough by steam train. The public toilets. were built over a disused gold mine shaft. It had a wooden floor and was very deep judging by the time it took for your excrement to reach the water below.

At Manus Island where there is almost no tidal effect, they had a long low roofed jetty projecting about thirty metres into the lagoon, opening to the ocean. Toilet seats were provided ten each side and the fish did the rest.

At Tacloban on Letye Island in the Philippines, the US army had a huge elevated cylindrical oil fired furnace with square holes cut in the sides near the top of the furnace and a wooden platform to walk on a little lower down. To use the toilet one would take up a picture frame like timber square made of 2'x4' Oregon. Carefully placing this frame over the hole in the metal it was a great way to dispose of the waste, but very hot! On the way out, the frame was hung at the bottom of the stairs. The washbasins were upturned GI Steel helmets.

In November 1945, in Manila, I was asked to fly to Hong Kong to bring out women who had been interned by the Japanese in Stanley Camp. Little information was available about Hong Kong but I was provided with some naval maps of the harbour and a vertical profile map of the islands and the harbour entrance. Most of the flight from Manila was by dead reckoning as there were no navigation aids. In heavy, overcast conditions we descended very early over the South China Sea and proceeded visually at 1000 feet, picking up the entrance to the harbour using the marine profile chart.

The Royal Navy aircraft carrier 'Victorious' (if I remember the name correctly) was in the harbour and gave us wind speed and direction. The small pre-war Kai Tak airfield was then located close against hills northwest of the harbour. After landing we found that there were unarmed Japanese troops everywhere, bowing to us whenever we passed.

I stayed at a small hotel (near the Peninsular Hotel) that was in quite a shambles after a recent final fling by Japanese Officers. I spent the following day seeing as much as possible of mainland Hong Kong and left the next day with a full load of freed female internees. These women were in a very poor state due to malnutrition over such a long period. I remember pointing out some beautiful islands surrounded by a turquoise sea to two women who visited the cockpit but they were unable to see them, due to their failed eyesight caused by malnutrition. I flew them to Sydney, via overnight stops at Morotai and Darwin.

'PADDY', 1945

It was a Saturday night at Camden Airfield, around 11pm, October 1945. All personnel slept in Quonset huts made from galvanized iron. 'Paddy', a huge fellow, had rammed a bayonet through the corrugated iron side of the Warrant Officer's hut, just missing the occupant. The Military Police from Camden were called in to subdue him. Our Commanding Officer set up a court hearing the next day, consisting of the Adjutant, an Officer Navigator, and myself. Paddy refused to come to our court so we had to hold the court in the Guard House. Paddy was naked, as all his clothes were confiscated. He refused to answer any questions and then began to work himself into a frenzy. He grabbed the bars and just pulled the whole place apart. We — the Court — departed rather rapidly to the Adjutant's office. The CO drew revolvers for us but as the war was over we all knew that we had not used them. In rushed Paddy, followed by the Air Force Police — it was an absolute circus and we began to see the humour of it, just like kids chasings. Eventually Paddy settled down and he became quite docile.

Two weeks later, I was taking a flight to Moratai via Cloncurry and Darwin when who should be placed in my charge to go to the Detention Camp at Morotai but Paddy. All was well till the first stop at Cloncurry. We had a tail wheel collapse and the radio went on the blink. It was very hot! We stayed at the old Post Office Hotel, waiting for spare parts to be flown up from Sydney. On the second day Paddy came to see me at the hotel and in his very broad Irish accent said 'Sirrr, I've a car outside which you are welcome to use to go anywhere you like.' I thanked him for his kind offer and later found he had conned the local Catholic priest into lending him his car. Where would I have gone on a stinking hot day in Cloncurry? We left after three days and Paddy got off at Morotai, like a lamb. I never heard another word about him.

In this same flight with Paddy, I had an English RAF Navigator. In the late afternoon on a very, very hot day we were sitting in our shorts on the veranda of the Post Office Hotel when I noticed he had black scars on his upper body and arms. To my query regarding these he said that he was a coal miner from Cardiff in Wales and the coal dust caused the black scarring from minor injuries. When I said how lucky he was to be away from that environment, he said that he was most anxious to be back at his old job after the war. He was deadly serious. This same type of thing had happened with my Rear Gunner on bombers, John Naylor. As the rest of the Crew had received Commissions and had become Officers, we were most anxious for John to join us. He steadfastly refused on the grounds that 'it would not look right' when he returned to his peacetime occupation of gardener on a large English Estate.

The war had finished and while I was still serving with the RAF out of Camden, in late November, I was having a few drinks with some pilots in the Long Bar of the Australian Hotel in Sydney. As it turned out, Qantas had accepted two of them and they suggested that I apply. I slipped around to the Shell House, Qantas Headquarters, and had an interview. I was accepted and was back at the Long Bar within the hour.

At about this time I received my Croix de Guerre from the French Government. I was discharged in Melbourne in December 1945.

RAAF Cert of Service

QANTAS EMPIRE AIRWAYS, 1946

In January 1946, I commenced flying Lancastrians, a civil version of the Lancaster bomber, on the Sydney to London run with Qantas. We flew the sectors Sydney to Learmonth, on the Exmouth Gulf, in the north west of Western Australia; then to Ratmalana airfield at Colombo, Ceylon (now Sri Lanka) and then to Karachi, India (now Pakistan). In those days British Overseas Airways Corporation — now British Airways — took over at Karachi, flying to Bahrain, to

Castel Benito in North Africa and then on to London. Day sectors carried nine passengers, while six bunks provided some comfort on night sectors for the very lucky six.

The Lancastrians were very, very noisy. They carried one Steward to prepare and serve the meals to passengers and crew. Learmonth had very primitive accommodation — canvas covered buildings with iron roofs, no air-conditioning of course, and the summer heat, day and night, made life difficult. Swimming in the Gulf was out, as sharks came right in close to the shore and patrolled up and down. As we walked they would be listening to the vibration of our footsteps and the fins would be seen moving along with us, turning as we turned. In 1946, a particularly violent cyclone destroyed the camp at Learmonth so it was necessary for us to stage through Perth. What a wonderful change! Crews stayed at the Esplanade Hotel, a marvellous old pub with excellent meals. Early in 1947 we commenced operating through Singapore, landing at the old Changi Airfield, near the infamous Changi Gaol.

The single runway was made of steel matting called PSP (Pressed Steel Plates). There were still large numbers of Japanese army personnel working there. The flight from Singapore was direct to Karachi, the usual flying time being fourteen hours. In the monsoon season, the all night flight both ways could be continuously rough — in cloud and rain all the way with no chance to get any star sightings — Astro-Navigation. As there were no radio aids, these were particularly long Dead Reckoning sectors and the BOAC crews did not envy us our half of the London route. For years there were no other aircraft flying on or near this route.

In 1948 with the introduction of the Constellation, Qantas crews flew the route all the way to London. Conditions improved, particularly as the 'Connie' could fly at higher altitudes; 6,250m for the Lancaster and 7,600m for the 'Connie'. I recall one of the early flights to London, landing on a Sunday afternoon at the new

Heathrow Airport and ours was the only aircraft on the tarmac. All the others were in the hangers for the weekend. Large crowds of sightseers were on hand and 'Green Sleeves', the current hit, was being played on the public address system. A small De Haviland Rapide bi-plane soon appeared and commenced taking joy riders on short flights around the Heathrow boundaries; a female ex-wartime Air Transport Auxiliary Pilot flew the plane. Not to be outdone, the 'Wimpy' Airport Construction Company put collapsible chairs in the back of their trucks and took sightseers for rides around various taxiways.

In late 1946, our Lancastrian was the only aircraft on the tarmac for a 9pm departure from Mascot airport. Under a very weak, single light stood two figures; the only ones in sight. I recognised them and went over to introduce myself. I said to the Prime Minister, 'Good evening Sir.' To which he replied, 'You don't need to call me Sir, I was an engine driver myself once.' I addressed him as Prime Minister from then on. He was there to see off Dr Evatt, who was making one of his journeys to London and then to Geneva where he was the first United Nations Secretary General.

Speaking of titles, I was in the customs area of Honolulu airport when a call came over the PA for 'Nuffield to report to Immigration' and his butler hastened over to inform them that it was 'Lord Nuffield' and the customs agent said 'We don't use first names here!'

QANTAS, 1948

In 1948, I flew to Singapore in a DC3, charted by an oil company to return some of their personnel, who had been working at their refinery in Sumatra, Palembang, back to Sydney. We refuelled at Jakarta, better known then as Batavia, Surabaya and on to Bali where we stayed overnight. In Bali, at that time, the women all dressed topless and proud of it, or should I say 'them'? As there was a war going on – Javanese vs. Dutch - the East Indies currency was bought for next to nothing in Singapore so we all bought locally made produce, some of which I still have. We stopped for fuel at Denpasar, Timor and stayed over in Darwin then next day to Sydney, via Cloncurry for fuel.

In September 1948, I left the Constellation fleet to fly DC3's on the Bird of Paradise run to New Guinea. There was no Radio Operator on these DC3's and all en-route communications were by Morse code, which in those days the Post Master General's Department carried out at the old and historic GPO in Martin Place. Duly certified, one became quite proficient at the Morse keys, located on top of the glare shield to the left and right of the Captain and Co-Pilot's line of sight. Apart from in the circuit area, where ordinary VHF (Very High Frequency) voice transmissions were used Morse was the major communications medium. Some sixty plus years on, I am still able to send and receive Morse.

A TYPICAL DAY FROM TOWNSVILLE TO LAE, NG FOLLOWS:

I would awake around 3:30am, have my tea and toast, and then off to Garbutt Airport, Townsville for a 5am take off to Cairns; flight time one hour twenty minutes with a twenty-minute turnaround. Then to Cooktown — flight time forty-five minutes with a fifteen minute turnaround; then a three hour flight across the Coral Sea to Port Moresby. It was essential not to run late as the cloud build-ups over the Owen Stanley Mountain Range could make the crossing to Lae very difficult. On some flights the next call was either Wau or Bulolo to pick up or put down passengers. The Co-Pilot would write the tickets and collect the money on these two sectors. We then went on to Lae. Once a week, there was an extension to Madang and back to Lae, arriving in the late afternoon. The next morning, I had an early call and then return to Townsville where the two pilots would stage for a day off, then fly to Rockhampton, Brisbane, and finally Sydney.

At Archerfield, Brisbane's old grass airfield, Qantas had its main DC3 servicing base, so we would change aircraft. All freight, mail, and baggage had to be transferred to the new aircraft. I can still see the bags of gold sitting on the tarmac, waiting to be reloaded onto the plane straight out of servicing. The New Guinea Bulolo Gold Dredging Company sent their consignments on the regular Bird of Paradise Service. No guards or special security arrangements — they were different days then.

I think Wau Airfield is worth mentioning as, being built on a hillside, it was notoriously steep. Immediately behind it, the mountain rose rapidly, making it a 'once only' approach. The technique was to approach a little fast, make a large 'flare', touchdown, then utilise almost full power to keep climbing the hill. We would then spin around at ninety degrees across the slope before cutting the engines and parking. The first Bristol Freighter to arrive at Wau on a demonstration flight by the manufacturer's pilots did not adopt this technique. Unaware they had to park at ninety degrees to the slope, the brakes failed to hold and the aircraft ran all the way down the field into a valley where it was wrecked, making an excellent 'donga' (house) for one of the local tribesmen.

It's amazing that within ten kilometres, just over the mountain west of Wau, lived the then very fierce Kooka Kooka tribesmen who were deadly with bow and arrow against interlopers. They were, of course, headhunters.

Three years after the war, I met my wife Hazel (Margaret Cameron) and we married in September 1948. Haze had the choice of an awful lot of blokes, because she was in charge of all the licensing and had to record them, so she met a lot of fellows. I was invited to a party one night, located out the back of a medical supply store. I walked into the place and it really was that thing where your eyes just locked on, and that was it. I must admit I was looking for someone to marry. I had come back from the war at twenty-two and by the time I got to twenty-three, all my mates were getting married. I found her and we had a lot in common. We spent the rest of the night together at the party; it was like there was no-one else there. It was about nine months between when we met and when we married. It was very quick. We got married at K9 — the doghouse. I think I invited about half of Qantas. My great aunt paid for it all.

Our Wedding : 24th Sept 1948

It was this same aunt who had looked after all of us after my father died — she managed to keep us all alive up in Maryborough by selling hats, Lady's hats. No lady would leave the house without a hat. No matter how poor you were, you had to have a nice hat. She was always inundated with people needing a nice hat.

Just before our wedding I had bought a little car, my first 'brand new car'. Haze and I drove it up to Brisbane for our honeymoon. The roads outside the city were absolutely dreadful. After the honeymoon, we returned to Sydney.

NEW GUINEA, 1949

Haze & Me with Lyse

The biggest event for us in 1949 was the birth in late October of our first-born Elyse Ninon (called Lyse). We lived at Newport, thirty kilometres from the nearest Maternity Hospital. A car-ambulance took my wife to the Royal North Shore Hospital with instructions for me to phone next morning. Fathers were most unwelcome until after the baby's arrival in those days. I duly phoned and found I had a baby daughter.

Qantas had a regular DC3 run — Lae, Finschhafen, Rabaul, Kavieng, Manus and back to Lae — taking mail, freight, passengers and fresh food to the coconut plantations. After an overnight stop at Rabaul the short sector to Kavieng, New Ireland, was made interesting by the very slippery steel strip there. During WWII the Japanese Army sent out some huge snails, about ten or fifteen centimetres in diameter, which they thought would augment the food supply for the troops garrisoned on the island. The snails multiplied at a fantastic rate and were everywhere after the war. On landing it would be one, great slush of crushed snails, making braking very difficult.

Speaking of oddities of nature and landing strips — Cooktown in North

Photo of Lyse and Me from newspaper article 1952

Queensland would send out warnings such as 'Large crocodile basking on runway' or 'Wild brumbies in Kunai grass alongside strip'. The latter occurred on one of my arrivals at Cooktown. The 'grass' was two metres plus high and just before touchdown a wild brumby raced out of the Kunai, dead ahead on the runway. By hitting power and climbing I was able to avoid the horse and land further down the strip. Nowadays, with more money available to airports, plus the advent of the tractor-drawn slasher maintaining a wide swathe of cut grass on either side of the runway makes the above circumstance something that could only happen in the past.

At this time, QANTAS had a flying boat incident at Surabaya in East Java. The captain was on his first trip in command, and during take off a current of wind change caused waves to steepen and the starboard float ripped off. The radio operator, who did the entire bow, berthing and drogue casting used to get very wet, so he was always stripped down to his underpants. He was quickly out of the roof hatch and made his way to the tip of the port wing in just his underpants, the boxer short type. Being a ship it was women and children first and the first was a famous concert pianist. She looked out, heard someone calling to go towards him, she did not like the idea, probably from what she saw and went to the easier starboard wing without the float, others followed her and in the end the plane capsized and was lost. It went down in shallow water, but the swift currents took it to deeper water and it was never found. All were picked up safely. It should never have happened. The crew should have done the old Greek method, crew first. The passengers would have all assembled on the port wing until a boat was floated under the damaged starboard wing.

In 1949 I had a most interesting neighbour, one Jack Miles, living opposite my home. His property ran down to Winjy Jimmi Bay in Pittwater where he once had a boat building business. His heart was not too good and he spent most of the day in his garage facing the street where I would join him if passing. He felt we had a common interest in flight, as he was a balloon artillery spotter in France in WWI — a very dangerous occupation. No parachute, and an explosive hydrogen filled blimp overhead that could be set alight with one tracer bullet. He would bring out a cool beer and cigars, both of which he was not allowed to have because of his heart condition. Jack had married a French girl in Paris during WWI and whenever we saw her coming up the garden path towards the garage, he would empty his glass and throw out the cigar, I really think she thought I was a bad influence on him as I was caught drinking and smoking each time she saw me. He was a good money manager, had quite a share portfolio and introduced me to the stock market in the 50's and it's been my interest ever since.

In 1950 the workload for pilots based in Lae increased rapidly due to the return of business to the islands. I was sent to Lae in 1950 to fly DC3's around the various islands and up into the Highlands. At least two DC3's were assigned each day to fly from Lae to Bulolo, load up with six-metre lengths of timber, and return to Lae. The trip each way took only fifteen minutes, but by road over the mountains and rivers it could take days. We would make many trips each day, the loading and unloading being the determining factor of just how many. It was during my time, on the Bird of Paradise run, that I was made Captain.

1950

My wife, Haze and our one-year-old daughter, Lyse, joined me in Lae in October 1950. There were pilots in Papua New Guinea who were falling sick and I was there to replace them when they did. I was living there for about three months before Haze joined me. She just bundled a whole bunch of pots and things and hopped on a plane. She arrived up there and things were really primitive. We secured a 'donga' close to the runway, the house surrounded by jungle. There were no facilities at all — no electricity or water laid on. The house had an iron roof covered with black paper (sisal). Forty-four gallon drums were located all around the house to catch the nightly rain. We had a kerosene stove and, horror of horrors, a petrol iron. This was the most dangerous piece of equipment, you pumped it up to get the gas, bloody dangerous things, they had a bad reputation for exploding. The clothes were boiled in an old-fashioned copper, heated with 'dee-y' (firewood). We had a very old native servant named 'Gunga Din', who lived in a tiny 'boy hut' nearby. We had to learn Pidgin quickly and Lyse became 'the piccaninny'. The shower was of the bucket type, the shower rose being holes in the bottom of the bucket. It was always my job to check out the shower recess (sheets of tin) for spiders, as Haze would not enter until cleared of them. Some were the size of bread and butter plates and they were many!

Haze and Lyse both contracted malaria though they religiously took Paludrin, the recommended anti-malarial potion. It always surprises me how different hospitalisation of small children is today, almost sixty plus years on. We took our little one year old, burning hot with fever, to the local ramshackle hospital where the Matron took her and sent both Haze and I away, which was the way things were done then. We saw her the next day but it was tough leaving. She made a recovery but Haze had recurring malaria attacks for the next four years back in Sydney.

At the same time, one of our more flamboyant, handsome pilots based in New Guinea, Nick, had married a most attractive dancer — Becky had starred in the chorus line of a then leading Sydney nightclub. Becky and Nick set up house in a jungle clearing not far from us at Lae. Becky tried hard to settle in but a large python snake dropped out of the ceiling of their 'donga' one afternoon and that sent her packing back to Sydney inside a month!

One day, Gunga, our houseboy, asked for time off to walk back to his village to bring back his 'Mary' (wife) — his village was high on the hills overlooking the Snake Valley about thirty-five kilometres from Lae. I asked, thinking she would be near his age, would she be too old to make the trip back? His reply was to indicate with his hands on his chest with all fingers extended downwards, at the same time saying 'Mary belong me, no old,' and then closing each fist and thrusting both thumbs upwards 'She young Mary!' The next day he was back with a large bandage around his thumb. To my inquiry he said a 'Sanak (snake) had Kai-Kai'd (bitten) thumb belong him.' A week later he took off again and arrived back with his Mary. She was young, and she soon had yams (sweet potatoes) growing and all was contentment.

On some of the flights we would pick up native plantation workers, accompanied by their wives, children, and possessions, including fowls and pigs. They would rotate with other workers for periods of six months away from their village. Pigs were prized possessions and it was the wife's role to rear the children and piglet. I was amazed to note that the breast used to feed the baby was normal but the other, suckling the piglet, was very large, giving a very lop-sided appearance.

1951

On January 21st 1951, on the regular Bird of Paradise service, which had been extended to Rabaul, New Britain, Captain Arthur Jacobsen (now deceased) was giving me my six-monthly route check from Port Moresby. We had reports of smoke coming from Mt. Lamington, which we could plainly see ahead as we crossed the Owen Stanley ranges flying at 8,000 feet altitude, in the vicinity of Kokoda. As we were passing the mountain, about five kilometres on our right, it suddenly erupted in our direction. We turned away immediately, diving and with full throttle to speed away from the explosion. When safe, we turned at right angles to the volcano and Jake took photos with his old bellows-type camera. The picture he took made the double centre page of the prestigious, American 'Life' magazine. All communication ceased as the static was just a roar in our headsets. A huge atomic-like black cloud boiled way up in the sky. It was half an hour before we were able to inform Lae of the disaster. There were two other Qantas planes, thankfully well below us, preparing to land at Popondetta near Mt. Lamington at exactly the same time as we flew over. They were DH Dragon bi-planes, based at Lae. The pilots had miraculous escapes, as the sideways eruption was not in their direction

Mount Lamington erupting

In late 1951 I transferred back to Constellations on the Sydney to London run. The only other airline operating at the time on the Eastern route was the French 'Aigle Azur' (Blue Eagle) we would see them quite regularly as we passed through India and Pakistan. This operation by the French Military had to be classed as a civilian airline to enable it to pass through and over the various countries on the long flights from Paris to Saigon in French Indo-China (now Vietnam).

Another eruption, Mount Egon, Indonesia from our aeroplane

Most of their planes were ex-Luftwaffe, tri-motored Junkers, with corrugated aluminium sides to the fuselage. Later, at Karachi, I was able to board one of their latest machines, the Armagnac, the largest airliner in service at the time. It was a four-engine giant compared with our Lockheed Constellation. It could carry 125 passengers and I was impressed with its huge toilet-washroom containing at least six hand-basins, all in a row. The principal use of the aircraft was the movement of troops to and from the Indo-China War.

1953

Another big event at this time, November 1953, was the arrival of our second daughter Melinda Marise (called Lindy).

On a Constellation flight in the early 50's, John Profumo was a passenger of mine from Sydney to Singapore then the next day onto Calcutta, then to Karachi. He was at that time Secretary of State for Air in the British Government, a most delightful person, a few years older than me. I have a much-treasured letter on House of Commons letterhead thanking my flight crew and I.

Lind – Our beautiful baby

Years later, in the 70's, my wife and I had a flat in Cadogan Place, London. I was assigned to fly the early Jumbo 747 flights in and out of London as far as Bahrain. We soon gathered that a high-class brothel was operating in the rear of the building by the number of Rolls Royces parked in the street out front. I happened to pass one of the girls from the establishment and she knew we were Australians. She told me that she was also Australian. I asked her if she knew Christine Keeler (Profumo's famed mistress) as I knew she lived not far away. The very attractive girl said she knew her well and that when they got very busy, they would ring her to 'lend a hand' as she put it.

I did another stint on the Lancastrians, flying our Australian wool bales over to New Zealand. This was a common trade, as Australian wool is soft and makes excellent clothing, whereas New Zealand wool is tougher and used for carpets. We would depart Mascot at midnight and land at Whenuapai airport, Auckland, reloading with bales of New Zealand wool and arriving back in Sydney about lunchtime the next day. This went on for about a month, with another crew doing the alternate nights. If it was cloudy en route and if we could not see the stars for navigation, we would have to descend early so we could see the land as New Zealand is rather narrow, making it easy to miss the island in the event of a strong unforecast tail wind. During WWII this happened a few times in the UK where delivery flights from the US had been known to bypass England and wind up in the North Sea. Our radio compasses at that time were very unreliable, in fact we used to call the instrument 'the butterfly wings' because they continuously moved and it was before the day of sense aerials, making it difficult to know whether the ground station was ahead or behind one's position.

WAR EGYPT – ISREAL (FIRST WAR) 1954

The diversion over Pakistan, Afghanistan, and Turkey was caused by the Israeli – Arab war which closed all the airspace over Arabia.

Beirut has 3,000m mountains just to the east of the town and in winter the prevailing westerly winds pack the stormy weather against them. A radio beacon was the only letdown aid. Very careful procedures had to be exercised during the letdown particularly as the beacon was of less than high standard.

The stopover in Beirut lasted approximately two or three days, thankfully Beirut was a great tourist city. There was plenty of sightseeing, water-skiing and snow skiing. Unfortunately, it all changed and Beirut became a violent place. By that time we were flying the normal route across Arabia and staging back at Cairo, living in the Nile Hilton Hotel.

OUR ROUTE AT THE TIME OF THE DIVERSION TO BEIRUT WAS AS FOLLOWS:

Singapore to Colombo – 7hours Day
Colombo to Bombay – 3hours 55mins Day
Bombay to Karachi – 2hours 30mins Night
Karachi to Beirut arriving at dawn – 8 hours Night 21:25 Flying time
Total elapsed time — 32 hours

QANTAS 1954

In the early 1950's flying the Constellations to London with 36 passengers we would draw their attention to various places of interest and as we were the only plane flying in that part of the world we could please ourselves about altitude and timing so long as we let control know of any great changes.

SISTER VIVIENNE BULLWINKLE

En route from Batavia to Singapore, a daylight flight, I invited Sister Bullwinkle to the flight deck as we approached Banka Island. She was able to identify the small bay where the twenty-one

Australian nurses were massacred, by Japanese gunfire, after being forced into the sea. Sister Bullwinkle played dead and got away, only to be captured later and interned with all the Dutch women, having to remain silent about her ordeal until the end of the war. If the Japanese ever found out that she had been a survivor of the massacre she would have been put to death immediately.

1954 SIR EDMUND HILLARY

The New Zealand mountaineer extraordinaire Sir Edmund Hillary was on a world tour following his successful Mt Everest climb. He was aboard my flight from Mauritius to Johannesburg, South Africa and approaching Reunion Island, I invited him to the flight deck for a better view of the island. He was particularly taken with the most famous mountain on the island, the volcanic Piton De La Fournaise. He expressed a desire to climb it in the future. I was very impressed with Sir Edmunds' unassuming manner.

KOALAS

The northern beaches of Sydney had very few dogs and cats because of the huge numbers of ticks in the area. At that time there was no tick antidote so the koalas were in considerable numbers, particularly as our place had a sugar gum tree at the front fence and it would always have three or four koalas eating its leaves. The noise they made at night was as if we had a pigsty in the front yard, much grunting and squalling. The tree was shallow rooted and blew over in a big storm and we were finally able to get a good night's sleep when the koalas moved on.

QANTAS CHECK AND TRAINING SECTION, 1956

As I recall, the Constellation training section consisted of only seven pilots. Qantas had bought a Constellation identical to our own four planes from the Irish Airline, Airlingus. Management were anxious to get the new plane operating on the line as soon as possible, with pilots converting from our DC4's to the 'Connies'. The planes had finished their day conversion but had to have their night certification and I was allocated to complete this at Narromine. A mechanical problem delayed departure till 10pm. On the forty-five minute flight to Narromine, I gave instruction on the radio magnetic compass, as this was a new instrument to these pilots, intercepting and tracking bearings towards and away from various radio beacons en route to Narromine. With a short stop for refuelling, a stretch of my legs and a sandwich at around 2:30am, twenty-nine circuits and landings were completed and the flight landed back at Mascot at 6:30am, just as it was getting light. Not surprisingly, after completing the reports, my drive home to Newport was much more difficult than usual because I was so tired. To my knowledge this all night circuit flying had not been done before nor since. Our total flying time was six hours and twenty minutes.

Over the next few years, flying Constellations and Super Constellations, I flew all routes, UK, US, NZ, Asia, and South Africa. During this time, Qantas operated an around-the-world service. In 1956 I joined the Training Section as a Senior Check Captain.

In March 1958, I was assigned, with Captain Ron Duffield, to fly the Queen Mother from Mauritius to London via Nairobi and Malta. She was travelling via Africa in order to open the new Nairobi Airport. Ron Duffield and I waited at Mauritius for the arrival of the Super Constellation on its flight from Sydney, Perth, and Cocos Island to Mauritius.

In the final hour before arrival at Plaisance Airport, Captain 'Torchy' Uren (now deceased) experienced an engine failure. After landing, it was soon obvious that a replacement engine would have to be flown in from Sydney. Two days later the engine arrived, as did a cyclone. The engineers managed the engine change under the most appalling conditions, out in the open. The Queen Mother's Equerry insisted that the engine be tested in the air, so in rain and low cloud, I satisfied this requirement. The departure from Mauritius was uneventful but over Madagascar, we began to experience ignition problems with a different engine and as Nairobi Airport had no Constellation spares we thought it best to land at Entebbe on the shores of Lake Victoria. The opening of the new Nairobi Airport by the Queen Mother had to be abandoned.

The engineers we carried, George Williams and Kerin Bolonkin, were able to repair the ignition system in two days and after an air test over Lake Victoria, we set out, direct for Malta, on an all-night flight. The flight was uneventful until about 4am, as we approached Malta, when we found it was not possible to get the undercarriage down by either the normal or the emergency system. By turning various hydraulic systems 'off' and 'on', the gear finally came down to our immense relief! After landing, leaks were found in the hydraulic system, making it impossible to complete the flight to London. After the flight, the Queen Mother individually thanked each member of the crew. Words cannot convey my admiration for the way this gracious lady accepted the various misfortunes, giving us all encouragement during that hectic week.

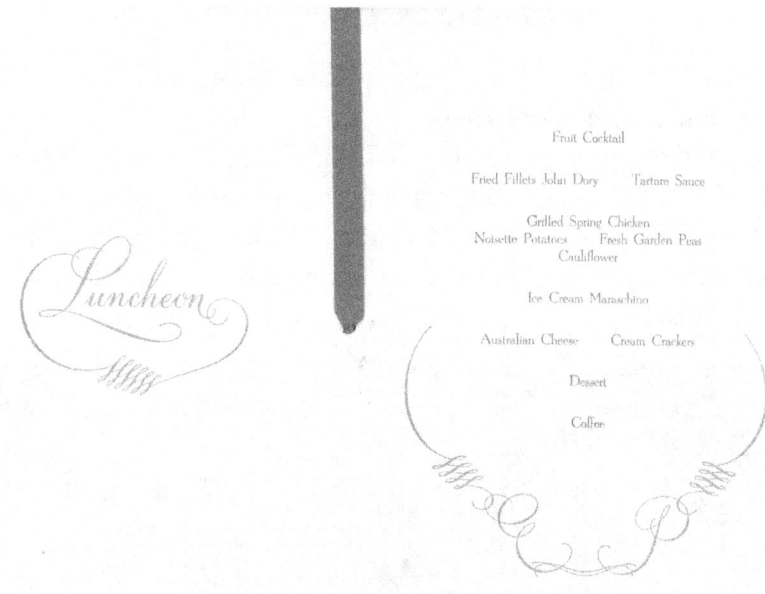

QANTAS Menu from the Queen Mother's Flight

With the Queen Mother at Malta

707 TRAINING — SEATTLE, 1958

In November 1958, Captain Eric Robinson, Qantas Chief of Training, Jim Pollock (both now deceased) and I were sent to Seattle to fly the prototype Boeing 707, known then as the -80 (Dash 80). It was a flying test bed, loaded with recording gear and had four different type jet engines. Captain Jim Brough, the Chief Examiner of Airmen for the Civil Aviation Department, was the fourth member of our party.

Training crew 707's Seattle

On the program of our first flight, Boeing had a Chase-Fighter plane closely observe the Tail-Plane (stabiliser) of the Dash 80 during various stalls. We had carried out some fifteen stalls when our pilot lost sight of the Chase-Plane and the Chase-Pilot radioed that he also had lost sight of us. Jim Brough happened to look up through a small 'eyebrow' window in the cockpit ceiling above the pilot's seat and warned that the fighter was immediately above us, and coming down fast. Our Boeing Test-Pilot called 'Break left!' to the Fighter Pilot and he slid down the left side of our plane and in front of the wing. A close call indeed!

The Boeing Aircraft Manufacturing Company had not produced a civilian passenger plane since the late 1930's. The last one being the Boeing Strato Liner from which they later developed the Flying Fortress; so the commercial 707 involved dealing with the FAA and Airlines directly. Previously all they had to do was test fly their product and the Military, Air Force, or Navy would do all the rest. There was a rush to get civil demonstration pilots. The pilot assigned to us, Harley Beard, had been an Air Force engineering test pilot, flying fighter aircraft. He had only three hours on the Dash 80 707 when we had our first flight with him. Seattle is not a high wind area of the US, but on this day, there was a near maximum crosswind for the landing. I was the last to fly and wound up in the left seat (Captain's Seat) for the landing. The 707 were very light on the aileron controls compared to the Constellation. The crosswind application was the same as I had done hundreds of times before. At about 300 feet, he decided to take over and land the machine. He had been used to fighter technique for strong crosswind landing and made a mess of it. We hit the ground left wheel first, going sideways. The left tyres blew-out, they unwrapped and damaged the flaps on that side. This resulted in the plane grounded for two days to fix the flaps. Three years later, July 1961, I was back at Boeing to give each Qantas pilot two hours to familiarise themselves with the modifications caused by the new fan engines. I went to the Boeing control tower at Renton to see what air space I could use. I introduced myself to the Flight Controller who said 'Phillips, that name rings a bell, you were the pilot who did the landing that damaged our precious Dash 80 plane.' I hotly denied the allegation. The only person on that flight still in the land of the living is Jim Brough of Sydney, then Chief Examiner of Airmen with the

Department of Civil Aviation who confirms that I had not done the landing! I mention this incident as this famous plane, and matching logbooks, now reside in the Smithsonian Institute in Philadelphia and some people will say anything to keep their job.

I might mention that the Dash 80 was filled from the crew door to the rear bulkhead with electronic recording apparatus. The next flight we carried out at least a dozen stalls in every configuration; flaps full down, gear up, gear down, all with a Chase-Jet Fighter tucked close in to our tail to observe the horizontal stabilizer, to see if it vibrated at or near the stall. Later on this flight, Jim Brough wanted to check the minimum control speed, with two engines out on one side and the other two on full power. On the Dash 80 there was no rudder hydraulic system fitted, the pilot pushed the rudder control tab to initially move the rudder then the pressure balance panel in the vertical fin sensed a pressure change and assisted the pilot if more rudder was required. Allowing the aircraft to climb slowly, reduced the air speed, requiring more rudder to keep straight. Suddenly the pressure balance panel stalled and sucked the rudder hard over to assist the two engines. It was a very rapid manoeuvre. A flick half roll, and going back in the opposite direction, all engines idled before control was regained and 2000 feet lost in height. Boeing fitted hydraulically controlled rudders on our 707's. We carried out all the above procedures at 12,000 feet altitude.

Qantas paid to get me a short endorsement on the Dash 80 type so that I could compare the handling with the simulator that was being built at Binghamton NY, for delivery to Australia, where I would be in charge of the new simulator for crew training. The short endorsement was carried out at different airports, Portland in Oregon State being one of them, and the new Boeing runway at Renton, about thirty kilometres out of Seattle, and of course the original Boeing factory field right in the suburbs of Seattle.

Back in Australia, I shared a training session of four hours with one of the Boeing pilots down at Avalon near Geelong Victoria. After two hours with my 'two students', as the Boeing pilot called them, I asked 'Anyone for coffee?' and I got three requests. I went to the galley where coffee was always 'ON' and I poured the coffee, put the mugs on a small tray, and as I entered the cockpit the Boeing pilot started into a perfectly executed 'One G' barrel roll. He had surreptitiously built up the speed to the required 350 knots by lowering the nose and adding a little more engine thrust to catch me unawares. All I saw was the horizon going through 360°. Not a drop of coffee spilt and I did not have to hold onto anything. Top marks for a prank well executed. Our small Boeing was a highly manoeuvrable aeroplane.

Article re: 707 Crew training

We spent the next three months at Binghamton. During that winter, the temperature quite often fell to minus 20° farenheit. Although I had visited Niagara Falls when in Canada during the war, I went along with five other Qantas aircrew to see it on a very cold day, after an ice storm. A large part of The Falls was frozen and the river below was frozen solid. I cannot remember ever being so cold!

The bugs were painfully ironed out of the new simulator, which was desperately needed in Sydney for crew training before the first Boeing 707 arrived. Assigned responsibility for all Simulator training after the massive Analogue-type computer finally arrived in Sydney, this kept me fully occupied for the next six months.

On a night flight from Singapore to Bangkok I had on board HRH Princess Margaret. She made a request to visit the flight deck to which I readily agreed. As we were nearing Bangkok and the weather was very clear I invited her to stay up front for the night landing. My invitation was accepted and she was strapped into the observer's seat, immediately behind me. After touchdown, reverse thrust is applied and the first officer calls the speeds during deceleration to enable the reduction of the reverse thrust, and wheel braking only applied. After we completed our shut down checks at the terminal, the Princess remarked on the rapid speed reduction on the rollout after landing. We chatted on until I had to draw her attention to the crowd waiting at the bottom of the stairs to greet her. This was a most delightful encounter.

In the early 1950's, my friend Dick Gilkes, no relation to Ken, asked me to crew for him in an Olympic class fourteen-foot yacht one Saturday afternoon, in races run by the Royal Prince Alfred Yacht Club on Pittwater. A large fleet back then consisted of about ten yachts - our fourteen foot sharpie, a Bluebird, Banyandah, a One Star Olympic class boat, a Dragon, a Daydream sailed by Jack Pritchard — who became our club commodore and the Brockhoff's huge eight metre yacht. It was a handicapped start, and this was the beginning of many happy years sailing out of RPAYC, Newport.

Jack Gale was the starter, handicapper, secretary, bartender (the bar was in a small room attached to the side of a dinghy storage shed), and he also operated the club slipway winch and operated the club tender to deposit and pick up crews.

FGY PTY LIMITED, 1960

Wal Killingworth, a pilot also with Qantas, and I decided to buy a fibreglass Bluebird yacht each. We were the first customers for Jack Morgan who proposed to make them. He built a mould and eventually we took delivery of the bare hulls and deck, getting timber masts made by a builder in Balmain, and rigging them ourselves. Jack Morgan went broke so Wal and I decided to buy the mould and went into business with another Bluebird enthusiast, Gerry Garrett, a stockbroker. The business thrived and we took in a manager, Geoff Baker, who proved to be very capable indeed. He offered to buy us out after we introduced the Top Hat Yacht in fibreglass.

We had launched approximately thirty-five Bluebirds and at least six Top Hats during our time with this company and the Bluebird, designed by Ken Watts, became known as the 'Holden of the Harbour'. Wal and I were very pleased to go back to our leisure activities and our main source of employment with Wal instructing on Lockheed Electras and myself instructing on Boeing 707's at Geelong at that time. Wal also had a little Vet Practice on the side, as he was a fully qualified Veterinarian.

On holiday in Europe in 1966 with my wife and two daughters, we boarded a Qantas 707 at Frankfurt for the flight to London. On this flight, my youngest daughter, Melinda, began talking to the lady sitting in the seat behind ours. She introduced herself to us as Lady Baden Powell, who at that time was the world leader of the Girl Guides Association. She informed us that she had experienced such wonderful hospitality in Australia, and insisted that we visit her at Hampton Court Palace for morning tea, or 'Elevenses' as it was known, when we could make time.

I had hired a car in London for touring the UK and we duly arrived at the gates of this enormous old building, built by Henry VIII and containing over 1,000 rooms. The uniformed guard had all our details and directed us to her 'Grace and Favour's' apartment, an extremely large and beautiful home. Her maid announced our arrival and shortly brought tea and scones. My daughters had been Brownies and Guides and I had been a Sea Scout as a boy. I felt extremely privileged to be shown a lot of Lord Baden Powell's memorabilia and decorations from the Boer War. He had been the overall world Scout leader until his death.

MERVYN RICHARDSON, THE VICTA LAWNMOWER MAN.

On a 707 flight between Honolulu and Nadi, Merv Richardson, a passenger, showed us pictures of himself at the controls of an early Farman biplane in about 1917. He had us highly amused as he described some of the flight characteristics of the Farman. He lived near my home at Newport and we met often with our common interest in aircraft. He spent millions on the manufacture of the Victa Air Tourer, bringing out to Australia an Italian Designer to plan and build the plane. A few Air Tourers were sold in Australia, but the whole project was eventually sold to a New Zealand Construction company who won a contract to supply the RAAF with this Victa plane. It became the basic trainer for the RAAF.

I flew Boeing 707's from 1958 until 1971. In 1968 I had a short posting to Mexico City, flying Mexico City/Nassau/Bermuda and return. My wife was with me and we had a memorable sojourn in these delightful places. I commenced flying the Boeing 747 Jumbo in 1971 and was posted to London to operate the early services London/Bahrain/London, again accompanied by Haze. Returning to Sydney,

I spent the remainder of my flying career, until retirement in 1977, operating all Qantas routes.

Not long before I retired from Qantas in March, 1977, I was flying a Boeing 747 Jumbo from Frankfurt to Bahrain on a clear, moonless night at around 30,000 feet altitude when some flashes of light went past, very close, moving in the opposite direction. There was insufficient time for any action to be taken and I reported the near miss to the Ground Control immediately. On arrival at Bahrain, they advised that a flight path for a German fighter aircraft had erroneously been cleared through the altitude assigned to me and in an opposing direction.

The subsequent letter from the General in Charge of the Luftwaffe, pointing out that these risks are the price we have to pay for peace keeping, cut absolutely no ice with me. This was my final brush with the Luftwaffe!

My total flying time was 21,707 hours by March 1977, at the time of my retirement.

So ends the interesting part of my life!

On retirement, Haze and I moved to Rouse Farm, northwest of Sydney, in the foothills of the Blue Mountains. This is where we spent nearly thirty happy years. Haze passed away in 2005 and I have since moved to Avalon where I live across the road from my daughter, Elyse, and have my grandchildren Scott and Rosie as well as four great grandchildren, Georgia, Zekie, Dexter and Havanna, all living nearby. My daughter Melinda (Lindy) is living in Bateman's Bay, with her three children Jim, Jon and Sophie. Life is still busy but I have time to remember so many events in what has been a fairly interesting life.

"the Tasker H Bliss Boys" at a reunion lunch : Great friendships were made on board seen here with Alf Payne, his twin John not able to join us this day and the Late Charles "Bud" Tingwell all from Melbourne

On the 16th November, 2014, The French Government has awarded several "Legion of Honour" medals to Australians serving with the RAF, myself included

Receiving the Legion of Honour from Mr Kader ARIF, French State Secretary to the Minister of Defence.

Back row: Jon Nedwich – grandson, Greg Cole - son in law, Dexter Cole - great grandson, Scott Cole – grandson, Sophie Nedwich – granddaughter, Christine Jobling - mother in law of Scott, Rosie Gull – granddaughter,
Front row : Jim Nedwich – grandson, Lind Nedwich – daughter, Self, Havanna Gull - great granddaughter, Elyse Cole – daughter, Georgia Cole - great granddaughter, Josh Gull - grandson in law, Zekie Gull - great grandson. Missing Danielle Cole - grand daughter in law.

Self @ 21

Self @ 91

FREDERICK AUGUSTUS PHILLIPS :
July 2014

FAMILY HISTORY.

I was born at home in Malvern, Melbourne, on 14th August 1923.

My great-grandfather on my mother's side of the family was Francois Hippolite Amoretti, born in 1821 in Ajacio, Corsica — the same village where Napoleon Bonaparte was born. Francois' father, according to my great-aunt Lily, was one of Napoleon's personal bodyguards through his many campaigns.

Francois became a ship's Captain, operating out of Marseilles, and happened to arrive in Melbourne at the time of the great Victorian gold rush C.1860. His crew deserted ship and set out for the gold fields.

Francois returned to France where he collected an inheritance worth £9,000 (a lot of money in those days). He returned to Australia on the ship 'Countess of Yarborough' and became a naturalised citizen so that he could acquire land. He settled in Bet Bet, near Maryborough, Victoria, where he opened a store as a gold trader and also ran a hotel.

He married my great-grandmother shortly after she

My great-grandfather Francois Hippolite Amoretti

arrived in Melbourne from Ireland, being one of the many girls sent overseas because of the Potato Famine. He went on to run hotels in Maryborough. They had five daughters, Louisa, Ninon Antonia (my grandmother), Maria Catherine (called Lily), Florence Emma and Therese Marion; and three sons, Joseph and twins Francois and Napoleon. Napoleon died at a very early age.

My maternal grandfather Frederick Harling was born at Amhurst, Victoria, in 1863, the fourth eldest in a family of ten children. His father, also Frederick, arrived in Melbourne from England in 1848, aged eighteen years — he was a wheelwright and in 1854 established his Steam Carriage and Building Factory in Maryborough. My grandfather took over the business from his father around the turn of the century, building all types of vehicles from drays to buggies. Henry Ford approached him to become his Victorian country distributor, an offer he accepted. However, the shocking roads, particularly in the wet, made deliveries from Melbourne most difficult, so after a few years — around 1915 — he relinquished the dealership. He went back to building and repairing horse-drawn vehicles. The business folded in the mid 1930's due to the Depression.

Fred married my grandmother, Ninon Antonia, the daughter of Francois Amoretti, and their children were Ivy, Fred, Sylvia (my mother), Ninon, and Jack. My uncle Fred (my mother's elder brother) fought in WWI and was a survivor of the torpedo attack of the troopship 'Southland', in the Mediterranean Sea. They were on their way to reinforce the troops at Gallipoli. He spent many hours in the water before he was picked up. He then fought at and returned from Gallipoli. My Uncle Jack died in WWII. Taken prisoner in Rabaul while serving with the Second/Twenty-Second Battalion of the AIF, he was transported to Japan as a prisoner of war when a US submarine, off the Philippine Islands, torpedoed his ship, 'The Montevideo Maru'. No prisoners survived the sinking. The submarine had no way of knowing that there were allied prisoners aboard. Jack drowned on the 1st July 1942. He was 35 years old.

My paternal grandmother was Rosa Barnet, daughter of James Barnet, the colonial architect of the period, 1865 – 1890. James Barnet designed many public buildings in NSW. Among them were the Sydney GPO, the Customs House and the Barrenjoey Lighthouse at Palm Beach, NSW, dedicated by Rosa when she was a young woman.

Following is an article which I found extremely interesting as it describes the days event. Reference: Sydney Morning Herald, 17 April 1880 with reference to Francis Myers, A Traveller's Tale: From Manly to the Hawkesbury, 1885

> "The foundation stone was laid on Thursday, April 15, 1880, by Miss Rosa Barnet, daughter of the Colonial Architect [James Barnet], in the presence of several ladies and gentlemen.
>
> The visitors travelled from Sydney via Manly, where three vehicles were waiting to convey them to Bayview. There they boarded the steamer "Florrie" for Barrenjoey, a distance of about eight miles. The visitors assembled around the flag-staff, which was decorated with flags.
>
> After the preparations had been completed, and the bottles containing the scroll, papers, coins and a medallion of Queen Victoria had been placed in the receptacle prepared for them, Mr. Grenville said:-
>
> Miss Barnet, - I have the pleasure of presenting to you, on behalf of the contractor, this mallet and silver trowel, for the purpose of laying the foundation stone of the Barrenjoey Lighthouse. They are implements small and delicate enough for such fragile hands, but yet in those hands they will be instruments for initiating a noble work. With a few light touches of this pretty piece of metal and a few taps of the mallet you will lay the first stone of a tower which will be the guide and safeguard of

many future voyages. Above the spot on which you stand there will arise a noble beacon – the silent sentinel of the storm-tossed mariner, the shining monitor, warning those who brave the perils of the deep to shun the more obdurate dangers of these callous rocks. It will be a light looked for and longed for on many a darksome night. It will be the star of hope to many a weather-beaten crew, and the saviour of many a storm-pressed ship. It is for you, Miss Barnet, to place the first stone of that tower – a task easy in itself, but noble in its association, and fitted well for a fair hand and a benevolent heart. (Applause).

The mallet and trowel were then handed to Miss Barnet, who laid the Foundation Stone, and declared it well and truly laid. Three cheers were then given for Her Majesty the Queen, three for His Excellency the Governor, and three for Miss Barnet. On the face of the silver trowel was inscribed:- "Presented to Miss Rosa Barnet, upon the occasion of her laying the Foundation stone of the Lighthouse at Barrenjoey, New South Wales, 15th April, 1880."

As months went on, the work of erection progressed, and after fifteen months, the lighthouse was an accomplished fact, it being completed on the 20th July, 1881. The building was designed by Mr. James Barnet, and the work was carried out under the guidance of Mr. E. S. W. Spencer, Clerk of Works, and Mr. John Kelly as Foreman of Works.

During the erection of the Lighthouse, two workmen were killed; William Sparkes and George Cobb, both of whom were buried alongside the original St. John's Church of England, Pittwater."

"The Sydney Morning Herald" [17 April 1880]

Soon after this Rosa married my paternal grandfather, the Rev. William A. Phillips. Their children were Houghton (my father), Henrietta, Arnold, Raymond, Frederick, Rudolph and Beatrice. Brothers Raymond and Frederick were killed at Gallipoli in WWI.

My father, Houghton Henry James Phillips, was born on 8th of October 1882, the eldest son of the Rev. W. A. Phillips at Parramatta, NSW. As the eldest of the children — they had a lot in those days — and through much hard work, he received the Dux Award of Caulfield Grammar School, in his final year. Unfortunately, my father did not like his father very much and this may have been a catalyst for his decision to immigrate to Canada and join the Mounted Police. My mother says he snuck aboard a ship when nobody was looking. This was common back then, and when a stowaway was discovered aboard a ship, and if he was a young strapping fellow, they would make him work for the crew. I think that is how he gained passage to Canada. He certainly did not have a job. He became a Mountie straight away and went to serve in Yellow Knife.

He joined the North West Mounted Police (not then the 'Royal') on the 4th of November 1903, in Canada. He served at Regina, Maple Creek and Swift Current from 1906 – 1907 and again at Maple Creek from 1907 until the expiration of his term and discharge on 3rd November, 1908. His regimental number was 4089 and this must surely make him one of the first Australians to become a 'Mountie'. During his mandatory five years as a Canadian 'Mountie', my father obtained his driver's licence and travelled around Canada. At the end of his enlistment, he became a magistrate for an Indian Reservation. The mounted police probably would have elected him. He lived on the reservation and I would think he spent quite a lot of time with them; I'm not quite sure how long he maintained this position.

Following his return to Australia, my father purchased two large passenger cars, a Russell and a White, to begin running a passenger service based in Wagga Wagga, terminating in Deniliquin, by the year 1912. He met my mother when she visited an aunt in Wagga Wagga. They married in Maryborough in 1916 after he enlisted and had sold the passenger car business. With his driving experience, he was directed to the Transport Section of the Army and on arrival in England he transferred to the Royal Flying Corps. He maintained a keen interest in the early long-distance pioneer flights and took me with him to Essendon to see Hinkler arrive and later to see 'Smithy' arrive from the US in the Southern Cross.

1928 - Self with sisters Marie, Sylvia & Ninon at Seaford : all still alive in 2015!!!

We had a lovely home in Rose Park, one of the top suburbs in Adelaide. We had a maid, I had a wet nurse, and things were looking pretty good. Then my father became ill and of course you're no good to a family when you get sick all the time. The sickness had been with him for a long time and they removed the kidney, but to no avail; he eventually died of cancer of the kidney. He died right in the midst of the biggest and worst year of the depression - 1931. It was a shocking year.

We never saw any money really, at all. I lived with my grandparents for years. I understand why; you could not get any money from anywhere. People owed money all over the place. In fact there was an old man who used to go past my grandfather's garage door and he told me he would buy up people's bankbooks. He would pay money for the rights to their bank accounts. It was a common situation, during the depression that people would go to the bank to withdraw money and the bank would say, 'Sorry, not giving any money today.' This man bought the bankbooks knowing that eventually whoever had the passbook, would have them honoured and be given the money when the depression finished.

I was eight years old at the time of my father's death. My mother spent about a year in hospital after my father died and then had six months convalescence with her sister, Ninon, in Benalla, Victoria. She was left permanently lame with a fused left knee after many botched operations. It was at this time, my eldest sister Sylvia and I went to live with our grandparents, The Harlings, in Maryborough and our other two sisters, Ninon and Marie, went to live with our Aunt Lily, also living in Maryborough.

Although my mother applied many times for an increase in her War Widow's pension, two shillings and sixpence a fortnight, equivalent to about 25c today, but it was to no avail.

In 1934 my mother started a shop in Ripponlea, Melbourne, and she, Sylvia and I lived above the shop. It had very little stock – cigarettes, sewing needs and a few household items but mainly my father's book collection, both for lending and selling. A chance customer suggested that we market a new device – a needle for making woollen rugs with all kinds of designs. This started to sell and they thought a bigger shop in a busy shopping centre would be more suitable. So, another shift – one of many in the coming years – to Elsternwick and a large shop with living space above.

The rugs were made using the new needle and sold well for a while. The business partner suggested that he and my mother start a Patents Office in Collins Street, opposite the jewellers, Dunklings. I used to be highly amused at some of the crazy inventions brought in for appraisal. One or two were good but the overheads and the small capital saw the demise of that enterprise.

With so little cash left, my mother decided that taking in boarders was the only way we could exist. We had relocated so many times that I began to have thoughts of becoming a furniture removalist when I started work! Finally, I reached fourteen years of age and started working the same week as my birthday. I got a job with a furrier in Flinders Lane, the heart of the fur trade. I had to nail out skunk skins, imported from Canada, onto wooden boards and then carry them up in the lift to the rooftop to let them dry in the sun. I had to keep a sharp eye on the weather and rush them in if it looked like rain, which it often did.

After four months I secured a job as an office boy with an insurance company. I had to wear a suit and hat to work each day. I much preferred working on Saturdays, as we were able to wear a sports coat, tie, and NO HAT, finishing at 12:30pm. My pay for the first two years was 10 shillings ($1.00) a week.

As things in Europe grew grim and the Germans made life impossible for Jewish people there, some of our Jewish company staff from Europe arrived in Melbourne and were employed alongside us.

By 1939 a number of male staff were called up, as they held commissions in the Army Reserve. This meant rapid promotion for we younger office workers with increased workload requiring after-hours work – till 9pm. Our pay for this extra work was two shillings and six pence, about 25c, 'tea money'. In Swanston Street there was a café that provided a three-course dinner for one shilling and sixpence, approximately 15c, so we were in front financially.

It was from Melbourne that I joined the RAAF in 1941 and received the princely sum of five shillings, equivalent 50c, per day.

THE PLANES I FLEW DURING MY CAREER AS A PILOT

Tiger Moth

Harvard

Oxford

Wellington

Stirling

Lancaster

Douglas DC3

Dakota C47

Constellation 1049

Super Constellation

Boeing 707

Boeing 747

Following are pages from my flying log book for the period when I was actively flying during World War II.

F.A. PHILLIPS FLT/LT   WORLD WAR II OPERATIONS

622 SQDN. MILDENHALL   3 GROUP R.A.F

DATE	TRIP No.	TARGET	A/C TYPE	OPERATION DETAILS	No. OF A/C	OFFICIAL LOSSES	%
15.9.43	1	MON LUCON	STIRLING		120	1	
16.9.43	2	MODANE	"		127	1	
21.9.43	3	MINE LAYING	"	OFF BREST		NIL	
22.9.43	4	HANOVER	"	ENGINE FAILURE OVER GERMANY. BACK	137	5	4%
27.9.43	5	HANOVER	"	No. 7 TANK HOLED. VERY SHORT OF FUEL. MAX. ALT. 9000'.	111	10	9%
2.10.43	6	MINE LAYING	"	SPECIAL MINES IN BALTIC SEA	1	NIL	
7.10.43	7	KASSEL	"		113	6	5.3%
18.11.43	8	MANNHEIM-LUDWIGS-HAVEN	"	DIVERSIONARY RAID. SHOT UP OVER TARGET. No. 1 ENG. OUT. LANDED WEST MALLING	114	9	8%
22.11.43	9	BERLIN	"	No. 3. ENG. ON FIRE DUE NIGHT FIGHTER OVER TARGET. HEAVY CLEAR ICING CAUSED DESCENT TO 5000'. SHOT UP OVER DUTCH COAST BY ENEMY ANTI-AIRCRAFT FIRE. (LAST RAID BY STIRLINGS AS LOSSES WERE TOO HEAVY.	50	5	10%
				RE-EQUIPPED WITH LANCASTERS			
30.1.44	10	BERLIN	LANC.	10/10 CLOUD	440	32	7.2%
20.2.44	11	STUTTGART	"	MAIN DOOR CATCH BROKEN. DOOR OPENED IN FLIGHT. ON RETURN, INCENDIARIES DROPPED ON TARMAC	460	7	1.5%
24.2.44	12	SCHWEINFURT	"	TROUBLE GETTING HEIGHT. BAGS OF ENEMY FIGHTER FLARES. GOOD PRANG.	554	33	4.5%
1.3.44	13	STUTTGART	"	GOOD TRIP. HAD ONLY 96 GALLS LEFT.	415	3	.7%

No. 7. PATHFINDER FORCE — 8 GROUP R.A.F. OAKINGTON

DATE	TRIP NO.	TARGET	A/C TYPE	OPERATION DETAILS	NO. OF A/C	OFFICIAL LOSSES	%
7.4.44	14	LILLE	LANC.		40	1	
11.4.44	15	AACHEN	"		341	9	2.6%
24.4.44	16	KARLSRUHE	"	AIR SPEED INDICATOR FROZEN ON WAY TO TARGET. HEAVY FLAK OVER STRASBOURG. PORT INNER ENGINE OIL COOLER HOLED. HOME ON 3 ENGS. AT MUCH LOWER ALT.	369	11	3%
26.4.44	17	ESSEN	"		342	6	1.7%
1.5.44	18	CHAMBLEY	"	RAIL YARDS + WORKSHOPS DESTROYED. GOOD PRANG.	96	3	3.1%
6.5.44	19	MANTES-LA-JOLIE	"	RAIL YARDS	64	2	3.1%
21.5.44	20	DUISBURG	"		510	29	5.7%
22.5.44	21	DORTMUND	"	VISUAL RECENTERER	361	18	5%
24.5.44	22	AACHEN	"	RAILYARDS (VISUAL MARKER) 5 GREEN TARGET INDICATORS DROPPED	264	7	2.6%
27.5.44	23	RENNES	"	AIR FIELD ATTACKED.	78	NIL	
31.5.44	24	Mt COUPLE	"	RADIO JAMMING STATION ATTACKED AND DESTROYED	60	NIL	
5.6.44	25	D-DAY	"	NAVAL GUNS AT FRANCEVILLE, NORMANDY	125	NIL	
7.6.44	26	FORÊT DE CERISY	"	AMMO. DUMP. No 4 THROTTLE STUCK WIDE OPEN. PROCEEDED ON 3 ENGINES	112	2	1.78%
8.6.44	27	FOUGÈRES	"	RAIL YARDS		NIL	
9.6.44	28	RENNES	"	AIRFIELD ATTACKED VISUAL RECENTERER AT 1500 FT.		NIL	
11.6.44	29	TOURS	"	RAIL YARDS. BROKE CLOUD 2500 FT. BOMBED AT 2000 FT. ONE OF ONLY TWO TO BOMB, BELOW THE CLOUD. MY GUNNERS SHOOTING AT LIGHT FLAK POSITIONS FROM TIME WE BROKE CLOUD	75	1	

DATE	TRIP NO.	TARGET A/C TYPE	A/C TYPE	OPERATION DETAILS	No. OF A/C	OFFICIAL LOSSES	%
12.6.44	30	AMIENS	"	VISUAL RECENTERER. MADE 3 BOMB RUNS		NIL	
15.6.44	31	VALENCIENNES	"	VISUAL RECENTERER. RAIL YARDS.	92	5	5.4%
16.6.44	32	RENESCURE	"	FLYING BOMB SITES ATTACKED		NIL	
27.6.44	33	MIMOYECQUES OISEMONT	"	TWO ONLY LANCS. FROM P.F.F. MARKING FLYING BOMB SITES FOR 104 HALIFAXES (MASTER BOMBER).		NIL	
30.6.44	34	OISEMONT-BIENNIAS	"	DAYLIGHT. FLYING BOMB SITE (MASTER BOMBER). 10/10 CLOUD.	102	NIL	
4.7.44	35	ST MARTIN DE HORTIERS	"	DAYLIGHT. FLYING BOMB SITE (DEPUTY MASTER BOMBER).	100 APPROX	NIL	
6.7.44	36	FORÊT DE CROC	"	DAYLIGHT. FLYING BOMB SITE. (DEPUTY MASTER BOMBER).	100 APPROX	NIL	
8.7.44	37	LIUZEUX	"	DAYLIGHT. RAIL YARDS.	123	NIL	
12.7.44	38	THIVERNY	"	VISUAL RECENTERER. 10/10 CLOUD. DAYLIGHT. 'OBOE' TARGET INDICATORS USED.	222	NIL	
15.7.44	39	CHALONS SUR MARNE	"	BACK UP MARKER. RAIL YARDS.	110	1	
18.7.44	40	CAGNEY BATTLE AREA	"	VISUAL RECENTERER. DAYLIGHT. 3 ENGINES FROM READING OUTBOUND. ENEMY TROOPS AROUND CAEN.	942	6	
18.7.44	41	AULNOYE	"	(DEPUTY MASTER BOMBER). NIGHT. RAIL JUNCTION. GOOD PRANG.	125	2	1.6%
20.7.44	42	HOMBERG	"	VISUAL RECENTERER. OIL PLANT. HOT JOINT. NIGHT FIGHTERS. AIRCRAFT SEEN FALLING AT 14,000 FT. NO. 75 SQDN. R.N.Z.AF. LOST 7 OF 25 THEY DESPATCHED.	147	20	13.6%

DATE	TRIP NO.	TARGET A/C TYPE	A/C TYPE	OPERATION DETAILS	NO. OF AIRCRAFT	OFFICIAL LOSSES %
23.7.44	43	KIEL	"	VISUAL RECENTERER. 10/10 CLOUD TINSEL, CODE-NAMED 'MANDREL' FOOLED NIGHT FIGHTERS. LOTS OF FLAK.	629	4
24.7.44	44	STUTTGART	"	VISUAL RECENTERER. 10/10 CLOUD BROUGHT BACK TARGET INDICATORS	461	17 3.7
25.7.44	45	FERFAY	"	(DEPUTY MASTER BOMBER). FLYING BOMB SITE	112	1
28.7.44	46	STUTTGART	"	VISUAL RECENTERER.	412	8
30.7.44	47	NORMANDY BATTLE AREA	"	(DEPUTY MASTER BOMBER). DAYLIGHT 10/10 CLOUD. CLOUD BASE 1000 FT	692	4
1.8.44	48	NOYELLE AU CHAUSSE	"	DAYLIGHT. FLYING BOMB SITES.	777	NIL
3.8.44	49	FORÊT DE NIEPPE	"	DAYLIGHT. FLYING BOMB STORES	300	NIL
4.8.44	50	D'ADAM	"	DAYLIGHT. FLYING BOMB STORES	291	4
6.8.44	51	NORMANDY CABOURG	"	(DEPUTY MASTER BOMBER). WITH MASTER BOMBER TO OBSERVE ARTILLERY TARGET INDICATORS	2	NIL
7.8.44	52	NORMANDY BATTLE AREA	"	(DEPUTY MASTER BOMBER). GOOD RESULT.	1019	10
9.8.44	53	FORÊT DE MORMAL	"	DAYLIGHT. FUEL DUMP.	160	NIL
10.8.44	54	LA PALLICE	"	(DEPUTY MASTER BOMBER). OIL DEPOTS.	215	NIL
12.8.44	55	FORÊT DE MON RICHARD	"	VISUAL RECENTERER. DAYLIGHT. FUEL DUMP.	117	NIL
12.8.44	56	NORMANDY FALAISE	"	(DEPUTY MASTER BOMBER). ENEMY TROOP CONCENTRATION.	144	NIL
28.8.44	57	OUF EN TERNOIS	"	(MASTER BOMBER). DAYLIGHT. FLYING BOMB SITE. GOOD PRANG.	25	NIL

DATE	TRIP No.	TARGET	A/C TYPE	OPERATION DETAILS	No. of A/C	OFFICIAL LOSSES %
29.8.44	58	STETTIN	"	VISUAL RECENTERER. GOOD PRANG. LONG TRIP 9 HRS. 10 mins. LOTS OF FLAK.	402	23 5.7%
3.9.44	59	VENLO	"	VISUAL RECENTERER. DAYLIGHT. AIRFIELD	100	1
5.9.44	60	LE HAVRE	"	(DEPUTY MASTER BOMBER). GOOD PRANG.	348	NIL
6.9.44	61	EMDEN	"	VISUAL RECENTERER. DAYLIGHT	181	1
7.9.44	62	LE HAVRE	"	(DEPUTY MASTER BOMBER). POOR VISIBILITY. RAID ABANDONED.	272	NIL
10.9.44	63	LE HAVRE	"	(DEPUTY MASTER BOMBER). DAYLIGHT. ACCURATE BOMBING.	992	NIL
10.9.44	64	LE HAVRE	"	(DEPUTY MASTER BOMBER). DAYLIGHT. ACCURATE BOMBING. SECOND TRIP ON SAME DAY.	992	NIL

NOTE: No. 7 SQDN. HAD
THE THIRD HIGHEST LOSS
RATE IN BOMBER COMMAND.

AS MASTER BOMBER AND
DEPUTY MASTER BOMBER,
TIME OVER TARGET
VARIED FROM 10-20 MINS.

F A. PHILLIPS
F.LT / LT.

R.A.F. TRANSPORT COMMAND.
STONEY CROSS. HANTS.

23.12.44	WELLINGTON 1ᶜ. 3 FLIGHTS ONLY. AIR MINISTRY CANCELLED ALL OPERATIONS WITH PASSENGERS. THE 1ᶜ WAS UNABLE TO HOLD HEIGHT ON ONE ENGINE DUE TO NON-FEATHERING PROPELLERS.

R.A.F. 243 SQUADRON
MERRYFIELD. SOMERSET.

Date	Notes	HRS	MIN
10.1.45	CONVERTED TO DAKOTAS (D.C.3.)		
7.3.45	LEFT MERRYFIELD. DROVE TO GREENOCK, SCOTLAND.		
10.3.45	BOARDED Q.E.1. TO NEW YORK.		
26.3.45	R.A.F. AT DORVAL AIRPORT, MONTREAL. 20 HRS. LINK RADIO RANGE FLYING PRIOR TO FLYING RADIO RANGE ROUTE AROUND U.S.A.		
4.4.45	DEPARTED MONTREAL FOR SYDNEY, AUSTRALIA, DAKOTA KN369. LANDED ELIZABETH CITY, VIRGINIA.	5	30
5.4.45	ELIZABETH CITY TO DALLAS, TEXAS.	9	20
6.4.45	DALLAS TO SACRAMENTO, CALIFORNIA, VIA EL PASO PASS	9	50
9.4.45	SACRAMENTO TO HONOLULU.	14	35
12.4.45	HONOLULU TO CANTON ISLAND.	11	50
13.4.45	CANTON ISLAND TO NADI, FIJI.	8	15
14.4.45	FIJI TO AUCKLAND, NEW ZEALAND.	8	10
15.4.45	AUCKLAND TO CAMDEN, AUSTRALIA.	8	45
	TOTAL TIME	76	15

PACIFIC THEATRE OF OPERATIONS

243 SQUADRON, R.A.F.
PART OF ROYAL NAVY PACIFIC FLEET SUPPLY TRAIN

DATE	A/C TYPE	OPERATION DETAILS
4.5.45	DAKOTA (DC3)	CAMDEN - MASCOT (SYDNEY) - BRISBANE - TOWNSVILLE - MILNE BAY, NEW GUINEA - MANUS ISLAND - BIAK ISLAND - PALAU IS. - RETURNING ON 8.5.45, ARRIVING CAMDEN ON 11.5.45.
14.5.45		AS ABOVE
7.6.45		AS ABOVE
18.6.45		AS U.S. TROOPS MOVED NORTH AND RE-CAPTURED LUZON ISLAND IN THE PHILIPPINES, OUR TRIPS WERE EXTENDED TO TACLOBAN AIRFIELD ON LUZON
19.6.45		
20.6.45	82 hrs	
21.6.45	35 mins	
22.6.45	FLYING	
23.6.45	TIME	CAMDEN - LUZON - CAMDEN AND STOPS IN BETWEEN. EACH TRIP TOOK 10 DAYS AND APPROX 82 HRS. 35 MINS.
24.6.45		
25.6.45		
26.6.45		
28.6.45		
29.6.45		
16.7.45	DAKOTA	CAMDEN - MANUS ISLAND. RETURNING CAMDEN 20.7.45
25.7.45	"	CAMDEN - MANUS ISLAND RETURNING CAMDEN 30.7.45
10.8.45	"	CAMDEN - MANUS ISLAND RETURNING CAMDEN 15.8.45 VJ DAY
20.8.45	"	CAMDEN - LEYTE RETURNING CAMDEN 27.8.45
16.9.45	"	CAMDEN - LEYTE RETURNING CAMDEN 24.9.45

DATE	A/C TYPE	OPERATION DETAILS
8·10·45	DAKOTA	CAMDEN TO MANILA, PHILIPPINE IS.
9 to 4		RETURNING TO CAMDEN 19.10.
10·10·45	"	
11·10·45	"	HRS MINS.
12		TOTAL TIME 68: 40
13·10·45	"	
14·10·45	"	
15·10·45	"	
16·10·45	"	
17·10·45	"	
18·10·45	"	
19·10·45	"	
19·11·45	"	CAMDEN TO HONG KONG
22·11·45		RETURNING TO CAMDEN ON 29.11.45.
23·11·45		ON 24·11·45 I FLEW FROM
24·11·45		MANILA TO HONG KONG TO
26·11·45		BRING BACK WOMEN WHO WERE
27·11·45		INTERNED BY THE JAPANESE.
29·11·45		
29·11·45		LAST FLIGHT WITH R.A.F.

DISCHARGED IN MELBOURNE.
DECEMBER 1945.

www.ingramcontent.com/pod-product-compliance
Lightning Source LLC
Chambersburg PA
CBHW070337230426
43663CB00011B/2353